Cars

Mac Ragan

Foreword by Jay Leno

Featuring cars from the collection of Lance Joseph

Dedication
To all Hot Wheels collectors who take their cars out *of the package.*

First published in 2001 by MBI Publishing Company
Galtier Plaza, Suite 200, 380 Jackson Street
St. Paul, MN 55101-3885, USA

© Mac Ragan, 2001

All rights reserved. With the exception of quoting brief passages for the purposes of review, no part of this publication may be reproduced without prior written permission from the Publisher.

The information in this book is true and complete to the best of our knowledge. All recommendations are made without any guarantee on the part of the author or Publisher, who also disclaim any liability incurred in connection with the use of this data or specific details.

The word mark HOT WHEELS, the Flame Logo, the color "Hot Wheels blue," and associated trademarks are owned by and used under license from Mattel, Inc. © 2000 Mattel, Inc. All Rights Reserved. Mattel makes no representation as to the authenticity of the materials contained herein. All opinions are those of the authors and not of Mattel. All Hot Wheels® images and art are owned by Mattel, Inc. © 2000 Mattel, Inc.
All Rights Reserved.

MBI Publishing Company books are also available at discounts in bulk quantity for industrial or sales-promotional use. For details write to Special Sales Manager at Motorbooks International Wholesalers & Distributors, Galtier Plaza Suite 200, 380 Jackson Street, St. Paul, MN 55101-3885

On the front cover: A Race Team '67 Camaro (1998) and a '70 Barracuda (1997) pass through a Hot Wheels loop-the-loop.

On the frontispiece: The '53 Bel Air (part of the Hot Wheels Collectibles line) originally appeared in the 1999 *Lowrider* Magazine set. This light blue example followed a year later, and demonstrates Mattel's remarkable positionable suspension system.
Printed in China

On the title page: Note the intricately detailed wheel on this Shelby GT350 from the Jay Leno set, part of the Hot Wheels Legends series.

On the back cover: A 1995 Mean Green Passion and a 1970 King 'Kuda meet at the Elimination Merger from a 1969 Hot Wheels Competition Pak track set.

Library of Congress Cataloging-in-Publication Data
Ragan, Mac.
    Hot wheels cars / Mac Ragan.
        p. cm.—(Nostalgic treasures)
    Includes index.
    ISBN 0-7603-0839-X (pbk. : alk. paper)
      1. Hot wheels toys. I. Title. II. Series.
TL237.R34 2001
629.22'1—dc21   00-051113

Edited by Sara Perfetti
Designed by Eric Aurand

About the Author
Mac Ragan is a noted close-up photographer whose works have been featured in magazines, including *Antiques* and *Art & Antiques*; all of the photos in this book were taken by him. He is a member of the National Arts Club and the International Motor Press Association. His extensive collection of vintage and new toy cars continues to grow. His first book, *Diecast Cars of the 1960s*, was published by MBI Publishing Company in 2000. His third book, also to be published by MBI Publishing Company, is about the story of Matchbox cars. A native Alabamian and graduate of Auburn University, Ragan now lives and works in New York City.

Contents

	Why I Like Hot Wheels® Cars, by Jay Leno	6
	Acknowledgments	8
	Why Hot Wheels® Cars?	8
Introduction	A New Agenda for Toy Cars	11
Chapter 1	1968–1972: The Spectraflame Years	17
Chapter 2	1973–1977: Enamels, Flying Colors, and the End of Redlines	39
Chapter 3	1978–1981: Entering the Second Decade	55
Chapter 4	1982–1988: Approaching 20 Years of Production	67
Chapter 5	1989–1994: Upmarket Experiments	85
Chapter 6	1995–Present: Reaching the Adult Collector	101
Appendices	Buying Hot Wheels® Cars	124
	Resources	124
	Price Guide	125
	Index	128

Why I Like Hot Wheels® Cars

**by Jay Leno,
host of NBC-TV's** *The Tonight Show*

Some people may be wondering why I've chosen to write the foreword to Mac Ragan's book on Hot Wheels cars. That's easy. First of all, it's no secret that I love cars, mostly real ones. But I also can admire toy cars and Mac Ragan is as passionate and knowledgeable about 1/64th-scale cars as anyone I've come across. Furthermore, it seems that Mattel, makers of Hot Wheels cars, loves the real cars I own. They've made reproductions of some of my favorites—a Jaguar XKE, Lamborghini Miura, Shelby Cobra replica, and Shelby GT350—which Mac Ragan includes in this fine book.

Let me tell you a little about how I came to love cars. Before I was old enough to drive real cars I had this great slot car track that my brother Patrick made for me. He was 10 years older and an accomplished carpenter. Instead of using plastic slot car track, he laid out pieces of plywood on the floor, took a router, and cut a groove in the surface of the wood. Then we put down wires on each side of the slot for the electrical connection and used a special paint that had grip to it to keep the cars from sliding off the track. So on my track, the cars didn't go clickety, clickety, clickety like on every other kid's plastic tracks because there were no joints to cross! My setup was one, long, unbreakable track. Then we did the whole thing up with lichen bushes and a plastic gas station and all sorts of realistic details. We even built our own slot cars. It was all really cool and so much more fun to me than playing with regular toy cars.

Then I discovered all those plastic model Revell Ed "Big Daddy" Roth kits. My brother, the carpenter, was also a master model builder. His finished models were always so good—detailed to the point where they were show-quality. That's where we differed. I was the anxious kid. I'd glue the kit together and then spray paint it. I'd do everything totally wrong. The car would end up with blue wheels and a partly painted windshield. A year or so later I'd be putting gasoline and an M-80 in the back seat of the model and setting it on fire. That's what happened to the Munster model.

I had the Visible V-8 kit too, which was a large-scale model with a clear engine block that let you see how the insides worked. All the other guys wanted the Visible Woman, but I wanted the V-8. Anyway, you could only tell she was the Visible Woman because she had long hair. Anatomically it seemed like she had the same equipment as the Visible Guy!

After these kits I graduated to go-karts. I grew up in Andover, Massachusetts, which at that time was pretty rural. I was lucky to grow up with a lot of land around the house. By the time I was 12, some neighbor friends and I bought a real car—an old Renault 4CV. We made a track in the field by our house and we used to drive that thing around and around. When you're in rural farm country, I think there's nothing wrong with playing with cars. My mom could look out the window and there we were, just driving around—not particularly fast, since the car only had about 23 horsepower.

My trouble now is that every time I go to buy a model car I stop and think, hey, you've got real cars that are broken and need to be put together, so what are you doing looking at miniature plastic Chevrolets and Pontiacs? I do, however, own many cars put out by the Franklin Mint. When the Hot Wheels people approached me about reproducing some of my real cars, I picked out some I thought were really interesting—Duesenbergs and Bugattis. But they said, "Our audience isn't going to know what they are." Let's face it, kids today don't have much connection to those cars. So I invited the Mattel folks over to my garage and let them pick out the cars they thought were best suited for their market.

I like cars and I think anything that encourages people to get interested in them is good. When I was a kid, everything was cars and hot rods—now, for many kids, it's the Internet. On occasion, I invite kids from the Pasadena School of Design to come over and drive my cars. Although there are a lot of fine cars in first-rate museums, such as those at L.A.'s Petersen Automotive Museum, there aren't many places that let people actually get in and drive the vehicles. People hear that the Duesenberg was the supercar of the day. Well, you have to get in and drive one to realize there is a little truth and a little lie to that myth. I mean they're great fun to drive and they were faster than anything else you could get at the time, but they're not fast compared to modern cars.

I like the whole spectrum of cars and I think that if you're someone who collects something eventually you're going to reach back as far as you can. For instance, when I was 16, I couldn't imagine why anybody would want a '32 Ford when you could drive a GTO. Well, now I like the '32 Ford because it was the first popular V-8. Hot Wheels makes a '32 Ford, as well as just about everything else—from Duesenbergs and Packards to contemporary concept cars. That's one reason I like what they do.

Mattel was extremely skillful about the cars from my collection that they reproduced. The reason they call my XKE the "Custom" Jaguar XKE is because, from the firewall forward, it's a '72 model with a V-12. The back of the car is a '63. It's a car the factory never built, but Mattel got it just right.

But if you're 6 years old, you're probably more interested in the car that "The Rock" has or whatever the hot thing is for kids now. That's what's so great about Hot Wheels—no cars are off limits—from classics to cars that a 6-year-old (or in my case, a 50-year-old) would like.

Mac Ragan did an amazing job in this book of capturing that eclectic spirit of the Hot Wheels car. He chose all of the cars so carefully—giving the reader a mini lesson in car history. But it's his photos that really make this book special. Thanks, Mac, for taking me on a colorful tour of my favorite passion: cars. Now, if only I could drive some of those Hot Wheels cars. . . .

Mattel perfectly replicated the aggressive face of the Lamborghini Miura, part of Mattel's four-car set of models of real cars owned by Leno. The other three vehicles are a white Shelby GT350, a red Jaguar XKE convertible, and a dark blue Shelby Cobra replica.

Acknowledgments

For this book I relied on the expertise and opinions of many people in the world of toy cars, and there are too many to thank in one place. I'd like to extend a special thanks to the following people:

Collector Lance Joseph volunteered his collection for photography and shared his vast knowledge of Hot Wheels cars, making this book a pleasure to photograph and write. Jack Sparks and Richard Gaab provided me with a free place to stay and work while photographing Joseph's collection in Miami. Larry Wood, Jim Wagner, Sara Rosales, Michael Dewart, and Tami Cole, all from Mattel, cheerfully fielded my Hot Wheels-related questions for more than a year. Sara Perfetti and Amy Glaser, my MBI Publishing Company editors, patiently endured my lengthy explanations of why specific—often esoteric—Hot Wheels facts must be included.

I am particularly grateful to both my father, who kindled my passionate interest in cars by buying for me my first toy car and my first real car, and my mother, a professional photographer and art professor, whose expertise and advice helped make the photographs in this book an accurate and high-quality photographic record of Hot Wheels cars. My godfather, Frank Mathews, has been a constant source of support throughout this project and my entire life.

Special thanks go to Ken Gross, noted automotive author and former director of the Petersen Automotive Museum in Los Angeles, who continues to encourage my efforts to document the history of toy cars; Paul Gottlieb of Harry N. Abrams, Inc., who taught me the best ways to publish fine, illustrated books; and David Masello, whose encouragement and guidance helped make this book possible

Why Hot Wheels® Cars?

From their tiny mag wheels to their brightly colored, funky paint designs, Hot Wheels cars are a special breed of toy. Their unrestrained styling and the tremendous variety of models—more than 600 castings to date—provide children with a complete world of vehicles: fantasy racers, trucks, and everyday cars. No other brand has ever come close to duplicating the Hot Wheels style.

You don't have to be a Hot Wheels collector to appreciate the styling and keen sense of humor found in these little toy cars. This book is the first to feature Hot Wheels cars in oversized, vibrant, close-up color photographs, combined with descriptive text. Many of the photographs show the toys as children see them—up close and at eye level, as big as real cars. Special efforts were made to highlight the features that make the cars so appealing—hoods and doors that open, bizarre custom alterations, and whimsical decorations that might include comic book characters or classic hot rod flames. While other books serve as excellent

This battery-powered 2-Way Super-Charger from 1970 kept Hot Wheels cars moving around the track by squeezing them between rapidly spinning foam wheels and projecting them out at a high rate of speed. Top level: 1995 Mean Green Passion, 1969 Indy Eagle, 1982 Sunagon; bottom level: 1997's '70 Plymouth Barracuda Convertible and a 1970 King 'Kuda. Although pictured in Mattel's own catalogue illustration, the Indy Eagle, as well as other open-wheeled Grand Prix cars from 1969, never performed well in the Super-Charger. Their lack of body structure gave the foam wheels nothing to grip. Thank you, Tom Lowe, for remembering that important piece of Hot Wheels history.

reference guides documenting the hundreds of Hot Wheels models, this one presents a year-by-year history of the important cars and trends that stand out as Hot Wheels milestones. Now that the brand is more than 30 years old, it's time to look back and celebrate the many models that have made "Hot Wheels" a household phrase among children and adults. Hot Wheels cars remain America's most popular toy vehicle.

In this book, pictures and captions relate surprising facts about the cars we played with as children and help us better appreciate Mattel's extraordinary efforts in designing these seemingly simple toys. More details about the cars are found in the carefully researched text: how and why the cars differ from other brands of 1/64th-scale vehicles, comments from collectors (adults and even 5-year-olds), and insights into the design process.

The cars photographed from the first 20 years of Hot Wheels production (1968–1988) came from the collection of Lance Joseph, one of the world's most important collectors of Hot Wheels cars. (Later models, from 1989 to the present, are from my personal collection.) Joseph volunteered his vast collection, generously and unconditionally, for me to photograph. Upon entering his self-described "Hot Wheels Room" in his Florida home, I was dazzled by a wall of sparkling, rainbow-hued Spectraflame-era cars. Once I was able to process that startling image, I noticed stacks of flat-file drawers, each lined with a foam insert coddling dozens more Hot Wheels cars.

It wasn't easy finding a collection as complete and accessible. Some collectors concentrate on the early Spectraflame models, others collect vehicles from more recent years, and still others never take their cars out of the package. Not only was Joseph's collection complete (he owns almost every Hot Wheels variation ever made), but the vehicles were out of the package and in mint or excellent condition. I photographed his cars over a 10-day period, picking up a new batch every couple of days for a trip to my photography studio. He gave me the time needed to discern each car's most interesting feature, which resulted in more intriguing photographs. Handling someone else's collection can be fraught with the constant worry about damage, but Joseph put things into perspective. "They're only toys," he said to me repeatedly.

Which brings me to why I wrote this book. I've always been passionate about cars, especially American cars from the 1960s. These were the cars I grew up with and admired as a boy: Mustangs, Catalinas, Continentals. As a young child, I played for hours with rubber and plastic cars and pressed-steel Tonka trucks. I soon moved on to Matchbox and Corgi toys. Then came Hot Wheels cars. I still remember my first: a green Custom T-Bird from 1968. I was so proud that I carried it with me to Sunday school. I loved the customized musclecars and the early fantasy vehicles that no other company was creating. But by the sixth grade, I started to miss the realism that Matchbox and other brands such as Husky and Impy perfected in the 1960s. Already—even at 12—I was nostalgic for the toy cars of my early childhood.

As an adult, I started seriously collecting Hot Wheels cars beginning in 1989, but limited my collection to models I considered realistic interpretations of actual cars. I had missed the point of the Hot Wheels ethic. After speaking with longtime Hot Wheels designer Larry Wood, I learned that it was always their intent to produce cars that were modified in some way from stock. That was their objective. With this in mind, I found myself appreciating (and buying) their signature fantasy models like the Surf Crate, Radio Flyer Wagon, and Screamin' Hauler as well as my predictable subjects like the stock '64 Lincoln Continental, Ferrari 550 Maranello, and Dodge Charger Concept Car.

After agreeing to write this book, I decided to do a little preliminary research into the history of Hot Wheels cars. What I found was amazing. Mattel stayed true to its mission of creating toy cars with the details and fantasy styling that children, especially little boys, love. The company did it so well over its 30-year-plus existence that no other manufacturer threatened the market-leading position of Hot Wheels cars. During all these years, the custom cars in the Hot Wheels line have continued to be a uniquely American concept. Soon, I was excited about the possibilities of celebrating this phenomenon in large color photographs and a lively narrative history.

For those who fondly remember playing with Hot Wheels cars, I hope this book shows you a few old favorites and also reveals the creative design and quality construction of the toys you took for granted as a child. For collectors, my hope is that this book acknowledges what you already know—that Hot Wheels cars are objects with the uncanny power to engage children and adults in ways no other toy can.

—*Mac Ragan*

Introduction
A New Agenda for Toy Cars

It's hard to imagine that Mattel's marketing department ever had reservations about the success of Hot Wheels cars. In 1968, their first full year of production, Mattel scrambled to meet a surprising and overwhelming demand for the new toy cars. The first vehicles were made at Mattel's California plant, but by the end of 1968, a second factory began producing the cars in Hong Kong to keep up with demand.

By the late 1960s, small diecast toy cars (under 3 inches in length) were nothing new. Matchbox had been enjoying great success worldwide with its vehicles for more than 10 years, and Tootsietoy, the American inventor of the diecast toy vehicle, had been in business for more than 30 years. Mattel, however, was taking a risk, because its concept was completely different. Instead of following the traditional thinking of modeling toy cars and trucks after everyday vehicles, Mattel believed that models of customized American cars would appeal to children. The company also thought the time had come for a strong emphasis on racing and speed.

One-on-one drag racing, whether on country roads or purpose-built drag strips, became immensely popular in the 1960s. Rally and open-wheeled racing (Formula 1 and Indy-style) had been popular worldwide since the early days of the automobile, but Super-Stock, Pro-Stock, rail dragsters,

Early Hot Wheels cars were made in both the United States and Hong Kong. The 1968 Custom Camaros pictured here show some of the chassis differences between U.S. and Hong Kong cars. Note how the Hong Kong chassis on the right features four open rectangles, which expose the torsion bar suspension.

The Hot Wheels line emphasized the racing side of its diecast cars by producing numerous track sets. The Hot Curves Race Action Set appeared in the 1968 and 1969 Collector's Catalogs with the same photograph, shown here.

Hong Kong and U.S. versions of early Hot Wheels cars featured interior and exterior differences. On the right is the U.S. version of the 1968 Custom Camaro. Its taillights featured an unpainted trim molding surrounding each red-painted lens.

and funny cars gained widespread popularity during the 1960s. These were American forms of racing, created from our obsession with power and flat-out speed and the fact that our land was crisscrossed by smooth, straight highways. Such circumstances determined that even everyday cars could be faster and more powerful than most European models. Automakers actually produced cars that were able to compete successfully at organized races. The American musclecar phenomenon (1964–1972) was the natural extension of this obsession with drag racing. These trends involving real cars helped determine that the very first Hot Wheels vehicles and sets were geared to pair two competing cars on miniature drag racing tracks.

Elliot Handler is considered the father of Hot Wheels cars. He was Mattel's founder and Chairman of the Board when, in 1966, he decided that his company should develop a line of small diecast toy cars to compete with the popular Matchbox line. His development team included Jack Ryan, head of research and development; Harvey LaBranch, head of engineering; Howard Newman, part

This page from the 1969 Collector's Catalog showed three of the "Original 16" Hot Wheels cars: the Custom Barracuda, Firebird, and Fleetside. Mattel listed the exclusive Hot Wheels features–mag wheels, red stripe slicks, and power bulges, as well as the anticipated colors for each model. In reality, Mattel painted most Hot Wheels models in each of the 16 Spectraflame hues.

the design department; and Harry Bradley, a car designer recruited from Chrysler. Ryan actually came up with the name "Hot Wheels," a play on the hot rod theme and the technology involved with making the innovative low-friction wheels. Company lore has it that Ryan, upon seeing Bradley's customized El Camino in the parking lot, said, "Those are some hot wheels!"

The Mattel team recognized that most diecast models of the era were replicas of foreign cars. Matchbox, Husky, Budgie, Impy, and Mini Dinky were all British companies that mostly featured models of European cars. Austins, Rovers, London buses, Vauxhalls, Jaguars, and Rolls-Royces were plentiful but very few Chevrolets, Pontiacs, Mercurys, or American Fords were present. This was reason enough for Mattel to produce its own line of toy vehicles. Ultimately, Hot Wheels cars featured unmistakably American models and they were designed for speed, a combination that made them an instant hit.

In addition to an impressive lineup of American cars, the toys' most conspicuous difference was their wheels: simulated mags. They were created by molding spokes into a black plastic wheel and detailing these spokes with silver paint. Red stripes were printed on the tires, a popular option on real muscle and sports cars of the era. Rear tires were often larger than the front tires, effectively jacking up the car's rear end for a hot rod look. Cars were further customized with hood scoops, exposed exhaust pipes, and candy-colored paint.

An equally important feature was Mattel's innovative low-friction axle and wheel design. While Matchbox cars used axles that were 0.06 inches thick, Hot Wheels cars were introduced with music wire axles, which were only 0.02 inches in diameter. The fragility of these thin wires made it necessary to

Every Hot Wheels car from 1968 to 1972 included a metal collector's button featuring an illustration of the model and its name. This Sand Crab is from 1970.

develop a compliant suspension system to minimize axle bending. An ingenious torsion-bar design created from an extension of the axle itself helped minimize damage. On each end of these thin wire axles rode a small Delrin plastic bearing to which the styrene plastic wheels were attached. Mattel designed these wheels with a narrow raised ridge at the inner edge of the tire's tread. Only this edge touched the track surface, and like a narrow-width, high-pressure tire on a racing bicycle, it produced less friction and faster speed. After several years of production, the ultra-thin axles were switched to slightly thicker and much more durable ones. At that point the suspension was no longer needed and was dropped from production.

Within one year, Mattel changed the way most toy cars would be made for the next 30 years. Even venerable Matchbox revamped its line to include hot rods, low-friction wheels, and bright metallic paint jobs. Mattel guessed right: American kids were ready for a new kind of toy car.

MAJOR WHEEL TYPES THROUGH THE YEARS

Original Redline

Redline II, with exposed axle (1973–1977)

Blackwall (1977–present)

Construction I (1980–present)

Hot Ones (1980–present)

Real Riders, smooth (1983–present)

Real Riders, deep tread (1983–present)

Whitewall (1983–present)

Ultra Hot (1984–1995)

Construction II (1985–present)

Turbo (1989–present)

Lime (1993–present)

Five-spoke (1995–present)

Seven-spoke (1995–present)

Three-spoke (1995–present)

Hot Hub (1995–present)

Lace (1996–present)

Directional or "sawblade" (1996–present)

Five-hole (1996–present)

Star (2000–present)

Spectraflame Colors

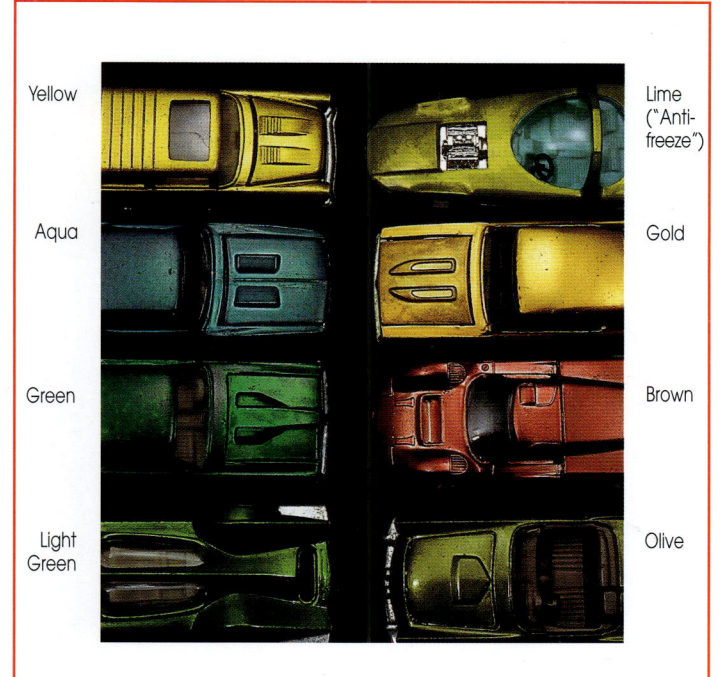
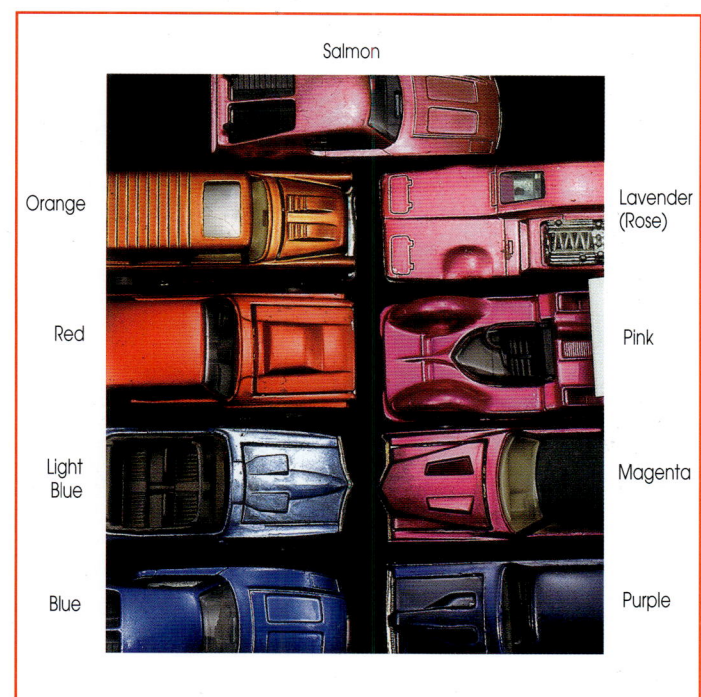

1968–1972: The Spectraflame Years

It's easy to spot an old Hot Wheels car—just look at the paint. The unmistakable Spectraflame coating on most models produced a finish unlike any other ever used on a toy car—a flashy metallic, candy-coated look that, when viewed in bright light, displayed a striking gleam.

The actual process was simple. The bare metal castings were not primed, but rather sprayed directly with transparent lacquer, colored with eye-popping shades such as lime green, magenta, and hot pink. True candy paint finishes are the result of two parts: a metallic base coat (usually gold or silver) and a transparent, colored top layer. But Mattel skipped the base coat of metallic paint and sprayed the color-tinted transparent lacquer directly onto the raw zinc alloy bodies (a mixture called Zamak). The metal itself provided the reflective qualities found in a metallic base coat of paint. Often times, more of the Spectraflame lacquer settled in recessed areas of the body so these areas became darker. As it dried, the paint also moved off of the higher areas, leaving them with a thinner coat and producing lighter-colored highlights on the high spots.

When they were new, Hot Wheels cars sported a look that no other toy cars could match. The colors were bright and smooth and seemed to glow from within—a result of the reflective quality of the metal beneath the transparent paint. Unfortunately, Zamak can be an unstable alloy over time. In its worst examples it becomes brittle, deforms, and breaks apart. Mini Dinky vehicles—the 1/64-scale line of toy cars and trucks made from 1968 to the early 1970s by the famous British toy company—are infamous for this unfortunate trait, and even the Hot Wheels Snorkel Truck (1971) fell prey to this unforeseen problem. Most Spectraflame Hot Wheels cars we see today exhibit signs of this aging process. Collectors and dealers use the terms "toning" and "spotting" to indicate that the finish of a car is marred by dark spots or entire dark areas. These are particularly noticeable in the lighter Spectraflame shades such as gold, light green, and pink, although if you look closely they occur in all colors.

As the negative aspects of unprimed Zamak became known over time, the days for Spectraflame Hot Wheels cars were numbered. Mattel used its

---

Inspired by the real car of Hot Wheels designer Harry Bradley, the 1968 Custom Fleetside featured a flip-up, hard plastic bed cover. According to designer Larry Wood, the real truck had aluminum drinking cups bolted to the hood in lieu of real velocity stacks.

Spectraflame paint created its own highlights by settling into crevices in the diecast metal castings. These areas became darker, while raised areas became lighter. Notice the ribs in the roof of this pink 1970 Classic Nomad. Like true "candy" colors, Spectraflame paint used a topcoat of tinted transparent lacquer, but instead of a painted metallic undercoat it used the bare-metal casting to reflect light outward.

1968

The 1968 line of Hot Wheels cars actually hit the shelves late in 1967. The series was an eclectic mix of 16 models. Eight of these were mildly customized contemporary cars, including the Camaro (considered by Mattel to be the first Hot Wheels car), the Mustang, and the Barracuda. Four were "dream cars" originally designed by famous car customizers like Ed "Big Daddy" Roth (Beatnik Bandit) and Bill Cushenberry (Silhouette). There were three heavily customized vehicles: a Chevrolet El Camino based on Hot Wheels designer Harry Bradley's personal car, a Volkswagen Beetle with a front-mounted engine, and a hot rod Ford Model T roadster. Also included was one true racing car, the Ford J.

While six of the customized contemporary cars were predictable choices—the Barracuda, Camaro, Corvette, Cougar, Firebird, and Mustang—two were

trademark paint for five years, until 1973, when the company switched to opaque "enamel" colors. Millions of Hot Wheels cars were made during the five-year Spectraflame period, but mint examples of these cars are particularly scarce because of their tendency to self-destruct, even in unopened packages. This is why collector values for mint examples of these early cars tend to be higher than toys of the same time period from Matchbox and other brands. There simply aren't many good examples left.

"In 1967, I was nine years old and growing up in central New York. We had snow five to six months of the year and a custom car was pretty much only seen in magazines. I used to read **Hot Rod** *magazine and would drool at all the California custom cars. One day I was riding my Stingray bicycle down to the local shopping center to look at the model cars. I walked into W. T. Grant and saw a new display of diecast cars. When I saw 'Hot Wheels with California Custom Styling' I went nuts! All these way cool cars with mag wheels and redline tires already on them. Blowers popping out of the hood, side pipes or Zoomies, and trick paint. I was in Hot Rod Heaven."*
—*Michael S. Zarnock, collector, Deerfield, New York*

A famous custom show car designed by Ed "Big Daddy" Roth, the Beatnik Bandit became one of the most memorable Hot Wheels models from 1968. This magenta version remains in near-perfect condition.

A coveted version of the 1968 Custom Firebird because of its matching blue interior (later models featured gray or cream interiors), the Custom series cars from 1968 and 1969 took popular cars of the day—Camaros, Cougars, Mustangs, and Chargers among them—and added features like side pipes, "power bulges" on the hood, and fat tires in the rear for a raked appearance.

Is the 1968 Silhouette the most remembered Hot Wheels car of all time? Bill Cushenberry's creation was a real show car based on a 1956 Buick frame. It featured a steel body and an integrated rollbar. Entrance to the interior was gained through the front half of the windshield which was hinged at the base to tip forward.

not. Mattel included a Cadillac Eldorado and a Ford Thunderbird, both large, heavy luxury cars. They, too, sported the mag wheels, redline tires, side pipes, and hood bulges that the musclecars wore more naturally.

1969

For 1969 Mattel evened out the mix. Ira Gilford, a former member of the Chevrolet design department, created the entire line. His first four completely original fantasy designs debuted in 1969: the Splittin' Image, Torero, Turbofire, and the now classic Twin-Mill, a concept car "powered" by two side-mounted engines. In 1993 Mattel introduced a restyled Twin-Mill II, featuring the requisite dual engines but now housed in a taller, more curvaceous body. For the 30th anniversary of Hot Wheels cars in 1998, the original TwinMill design was produced in a highly detailed 1/24th-scale Hot Wheels Legends To Life model where the head- and taillights flashed and the engines rocked to recorded music.

In 1969 Mattel also produced what became the most coveted Hot Wheels model of all time—the Volkswagen Beach Bomb, a customized VW surf van. In fact, two versions of the Beach Bomb were made. The first, a rare prototype, featured rear-loading surfboards. The more common model had the surfboards riding in pockets molded into the sides of the van's body. According to Mattel, the prototype was never sold in blisterpacks. David Espino, collector and author of *Treasure Hunting Collectible Redlines*, confirms that the early Beach Bomb was a preproduction model and that it was too narrow to work properly with the Hot Wheels Super-Charger, a battery-powered accessory used to propel Hot Wheels cars around their orange plastic tracks. According to Espino: "The rear-loading Beach Bomb was too top-heavy—it would fly off the curves. So the production model was made wider to work in the Super-Chargers and had a weight cast into the base to keep it from flying off the track." According to *Tomart's Price*

Arguably Ira Gilford's most famous Hot Wheels design, the 1969 TwinMill featured a sleek body with wraparound windshield and two side-mounted, blown engines. Like other Gilford creations, the TwinMill was designed exclusively as a Hot Wheels model.

Mattel included Collector's Catalogs in most of its track sets and accessory packs. This one, from 1969, measured 4 1/2 by 3 inches, and featured the famous Silhouette custom car on its cover.

Guide to Hot Wheels the prototype versions can sell for $10,000. In 2000 a rare pink prototype sold for more than $70,000 to collector Bruce Pascal.

Also in 1969, Mattel introduced the Grand Prix series, which included eight models of Formula 1, Indianapolis, and Can Am racers. Unusual because of its large plastic spoiler at the rear, the Chapparal 2G is probably the most remembered Grand Prix model that Mattel produced. Although these cars were available in numerous Spectraflame colors, Mattel made an effort to offer most of them in their real-life, nonmetallic racing colors. The Chapparal came in white, the Brabham-Repco F1 and Lola GT70 in British racing green, the Ford Mark IV in dark red, and the McLaren M6A in orange. These cars were well known at the time because of their exposure on television programs such as ABC-TV's *Wide World of Sports*, and movies such as *Grand Prix* from 1966. Mattel added two more cars to the Grand Prix series in 1970: a Ferrari 312P available in Ferrari-red enamel

One of the most talked-about Hot Wheels cars, the 1969 Beach Bomb has been found in two very different versions. The more common of the two is pictured here. It featured side body panels pushed outward to hold miniature surfboards. Its value on the collector market can reach several hundred dollars. Early prototype versions featured more realistic-looking sides and held the surfboards in the traditional rear cargo area. Unfortunately, this body design was too narrow and top-heavy to work properly in Mattel's newly introduced Super-Charger track accessory. The few prototype versions known to exist have sold for more than $10,000 each, making them the most expensive Hot Wheels cars ever made.

New for 1969 were four European models: a Mercedes-Benz 280 SL, Maserati Mistral, Rolls-Royce Silver Shadow, and Volkswagen Beach Bomb. Mattel kept customizing to a minimum; Spectraflame paint, mag wheels, and redline tires were the only obvious Hot Wheels alterations. Two of the prototypes shown on this page from that year's Collector's Catalog are of special note. The body of the Rolls-Royce looks suspiciously like that from the Matchbox Silver Shadow made during the same period, and the Beach Bomb pictured is the ill-fated version with rear-loading surfboards.

"I don't keep my cars in the blisterpacks because I'm of the opinion that these are treasures to behold (and hold), not to maintain in some 'time capsule package' for eternity. I've done my share of 'liberating' early Hot Wheels from their blisterpacks and have enjoyed the process."

—David Espino, collector and author of **Treasure Hunting Collectible Redlines**

Mattel introduced the Grand Prix line of racing cars in 1969. It included open-wheeled racers such as the Indy Eagle and this Shelby Turbine, as well as Can Am cars such as the winged Chaparral 2G and the McLaren M6A. Each was available in a variety of Spectraflame shades and in their original racing colors. The Shelby Turbine pictured here wears a prototype gray plastic clip-on spacer intended to help the open-wheeled cars function properly in the Super-Charger accessory. Ultimately, Mattel sold the open-wheeled Grand Prix racers without the plastic spacers.

and a variety of Spectraflame colors, and a Porsche 917 in gray enamel and the usual Spectraflame hues.

Since the line was already full of musclecars, Mattel added only two new ones in 1969: the AMX and the Dodge Charger. The first commercial vehicle, a Plymouth Fury police car, entered the lineup and has the distinction of being the first Hot Wheels toy to wear tampo printing. A six-pointed badge and the word "Police" were stamped on each side.

According to Hot Wheels designer Larry Wood, tampo "pad printing" was nothing new. Other products already used it—everything from toothbrushes and bottles to plastic spoons and hair dryers. The process allowed painted designs to be applied to surfaces with compound curves, like a toy car. An absorbent material like a sponge was used to soak up paint, which was then stamped onto the surface of the vehicle. Multiple passes could be made with different colors to develop complex designs. The same process for applying decoration is used today, although in 2000 Mattel began using a new technique involving heat-transferred decals. The image crispness and ability to produce subtle color changes can make the older tampo process seem crude in comparison.

In 1969, a personal luxury car was added too. This time the custom job on Lincoln's new Continental Mark III was less radical. Spectraflame paint, mag wheels, and redline tires were the only Hot Wheels touches.

The Ford Model T roadster introduced in the first year (the Hot Heap) was joined by four more classic

The 1969 Custom Police Cruiser, based on a 1967 Plymouth Fury, was the first Hot Wheels model to wear tampo pad-printing instead of decals or stickers. The model pictured here is an early prototype; later versions featured white fenders.

Mattel introduced four vintage Fords in 1969, including the Classic '57 T-Bird. This customized version featured fog lamps, a speedster-style cut-down windshield, an aerodynamic fairing behind the driver's headrest, and an opening hood that revealed a tiny diecast metal V-8 engine.

Fords: a 1931 Woody, 1932 Vicky, 1936 Coupe, and 1957 Thunderbird. According to Larry Wood, Fords were chosen because, "Well, that's just what old hot rods were." Like the Hot Heap, these "new" Fords were highly customized hot rod versions. The Woody and Vicky featured exposed metal engines, the coupe rode on tiny front wheels and large rear ones giving it an extreme raked appearance, and the Thunderbird had a speedster-style tapered fairing behind the driver's headrest.

For 1969, Mattel added three unmistakably European vehicles: the Maserati Mistral, the Rolls-Royce Silver Shadow, and the Mercedes-Benz 280SL. Like the Lincoln Continental Mark III, these three cars were left entirely stock except for their Spectraflame paint and Mattel's famous wheels. In some sort of competitive challenge, the Rolls-Royce went head-to-head with Matchbox's popular Silver Shadow, introduced two years earlier.

1970

The overwhelming success of Hot Wheels cars during 1968 prompted Mattel to start development (in 1969) of 33 new vehicles for the 1970 model year.

Ira Gilford designed the original Heavyweights series of trucks for the 1970 Hot Wheels line. Each featured an expansive futuristic wraparound windshield and headlights recessed in the metal bumper. The series lasted three years and included the Tow Truck pictured here. Look closely to see the battered nose of a purple Silhouette, collector Lance Joseph's first Hot Wheels car.

The plan included producing a group of trucks, called Heavyweights, and a collection of hot-rodded American cars, called Spoilers, featuring exposed engines and large front and rear spoilers. In 1970, Mattel also started the collector's club and began sponsoring the Snake and Mongoose funny cars, one of the most famous sponsorships in car racing history.

Ira Gilford cleverly designed his futuristic-looking Heavyweights trucks to resemble one another. They all featured large, wraparound windshields similar to those found on real GMC motorhomes introduced three years later. The Gilford look, however, was even more extreme: the glass area was larger and often formed part of the roof. An ambulance, cement mixer, dump truck, fire engine, moving van, and tow truck were the first Heavyweights. These toys were heavier than the average Hot Wheels car; they were longer and featured a diecast metal chassis and major body parts. Like all Hot Wheels cars, they rode on mag wheels and redline tires. Each featured movable or detachable parts: the rear doors opened on the ambulance and moving van, the barrel rotated on the cement mixer, the bed tipped up on the dump truck, the metal hook moved on the tow truck, and the ladders detached from the fire truck. Although the Heavyweights cabs didn't resemble any real trucks on the road, their functions—fire, garbage, cement—were obvious at first glance. In the Hot Wheels tradition, the Heavyweights featured an element of fantasy while also giving kids the functional types of vehicles they needed to complete their make-believe play worlds.

Mattel also introduced the Spoilers series in 1970, describing the cars as "souped-up super rods." These were hot rod versions of the same customized American cars Mattel introduced in 1968. Although they looked similar to the Mustang, Camaro, Barracuda, Firebird, Cougar, and Thunderbird from the "original 16," Mattel created new body and chassis castings, which included large front and rear spoilers and engine bays redesigned to accommodate a separate diecast metal engine featuring a tall blower unit. Hoods were discarded in favor of showing the complete engine. Wheels were larger all around, giving the cars a more aggressive look.

The 1970 Spoilers were the Heavy Chevy (Camaro), King 'Kuda (Barracuda), Light My Firebird, Nitty Gritty Kitty (Cougar), TNT-Bird (Thunderbird), and Boss Hoss (Mustang). Each was available in the usual assortment of Spectraflame colors except for the Boss Hoss, which was only made as a "chrome-plated" model. It was found exclusively in the Hot Wheels Club Kit.

The Heavy Chevy and King 'Kuda joined the Boss Hoss as special chrome-plated Spoilers available only in the mail-order Hot Wheels Club Kit. Thousands of children joined the club in 1970 and 1971. Along with the special car, the kit included a collector's annual (a magazine of Hot Wheels cars and sets for 1970), Hot Wheels stickers, patch, and membership card.

In 1971 Mattel introduced the Boss Hoss into the regular line and painted it in a variety of Spectraflame colors. A new Spoiler, the Sugar Caddy (Eldorado), also joined the series in 1971 and was distinguished for being more fantasy than racing oriented. The car's engine sported velocity stacks instead of a blower unit, it featured an opening hood,

---

"Hot Wheels were built for speed, and remain that way, even 30-plus years later. I can take my 1970 redline Mighty Maverick and probably beat almost any other non-Hot Wheels car in a downhill race."
—Neal Giordano, collector and president of the North Carolina Hot Wheels Association

and its futuristic roof was an extension of the windshield, wrapping over the top of the car and flowing back to a diecast metal landau section in the rear.

In an effort to maintain the racing image of Hot Wheels cars, Mattel sponsored two real-life funny cars in 1970: the Snake and the Mongoose. Funny cars, mid-engine dragsters with flip-up fiberglass bodies molded and painted to resemble actual street cars, were becoming an immensely popular form of entertainment by the late 1960s. Mattel saw an opportunity to use this trend to gain exposure for its toy vehicles. The sponsorship allowed Mattel to market Hot Wheels versions of the popular Snake and Mongoose. Like the real cars, each miniature wore the Hot Wheels name on its sides, along with the car's and the driver's name—Don Prudhomme for the yellow Plymouth Barracuda Snake and Tom McEwen for the red Plymouth Duster Mongoose.

The Mongoose and Snake also came packaged on their own special "Mongoose vs. Snake" blistercards, which featured a cartoon-like illustration of both cars. In addition, Mattel produced a drag race set featuring both cars and including enough track and accessories to simulate a real "heat."

Mattel introduced the Spoilers line of souped-up cars in 1970. They altered castings of old favorites like the Camaro, Mustang, and Barracuda by adding prominent front and rear spoilers, larger wheels, and exposed engines. This "chromed" version of the Heavy Chevy was originally available only by joining the official Hot Wheels Collectors' Club. Other Heavy Chevy models, as well as all Spoilers, were available in a variety of Spectraflame colors.

Mattel's most famous sponsorship, the Snake and Mongoose funny cars, resulted in miniature models of both cars. Tom "The Mongoose" McEwen drove the red Plymouth Duster; Don "The Snake" Prudhomme drove the yellow Plymouth Barracuda.

Another important first in 1970 was the production of two vehicles exclusive to a Hot Wheels set: the Sky Show Deora and the Sky Show Fleetside. Using existing castings, Mattel mounted a plastic ramp to the beds of each of these trucks. The ramp was used to launch a lightweight plastic airplane as the truck sped down a strip of Hot Wheels track.

Also in 1970, Mattel produced the first Hot Wheels promotional vehicle. The Jack-in-the-Box restaurant chain distributed the Jack "Rabbit" Special, well known to children from its role as "Bunny Car" in the Hot Wheels Saturday morning cartoon series, which aired from 1970–1971. The car, a special Jack-in-the-Box decal sheet, and a metal collector's button came packaged in a clear plastic bag.

Through the years, a handful of Hot Wheels cars became famous representatives of the brand. Mattel introduced two of these cars in 1970. The Classic Nomad's distinctive vertically stacked "quad" headlights and large glass sunroof helped make this car a memorable part of Hot Wheels history—remaining in the line, off and on, for more than 30 years. Another was the Demon, a model of the Li'l Coffin show car. This custom fantasy car featured a low chopped roof, which gave the car a sinister profile worthy of its name.

In 1970, Mattel also started a relationship with Tom Daniel and Monogram models. (Mattel would purchase Monogram in 1971.) Daniel is responsible for designing plastic model kits of legendary fantasy

> *"My favorite cars are the pure fantasy ones like the Deora and TwinMill—really any car that has been modified in some way."*
> —Larry Wood, Hot Wheels Designer

cars, including the Red Baron, Paddy Wagon, Sand Crab, Ice "T", and S'Cool Bus. All were introduced to the Hot Wheels line in 1970 or 1971. Only the Sand Crab was produced in a variety of Spectraflame colors. The other Daniel vehicles were produced in their original colors: dark blue for the Paddy Wagon, red for the Red Baron, yellow for the Ice "T" and S'Cool Bus.

Howard Rees joined the Hot Wheels design team in 1969 and helped create several new models for 1970. These included fantasy cars such as the Mantis, Mod Quad, and Peepin' Bomb, as well as two customized vehicles based on real cars: the Seasider (a Chevrolet pickup truck with a detachable plastic boat designed to fit seamlessly in the bed) and the Mighty Maverick. Along with new models from Ira Gilford (the Heavyweights truck series, the Spoilers series, Power Pad, and Swingin' Wing), the Hot Wheels line featured cars from two new designers: Paul Tam (Whip Creamer) and Larry Wood (Tri Baby). Although Tam continued to design Hot Wheels cars

The Jack-in-the-Box restaurant chain distributed the first promotional Hot Wheels car in 1970. Unlike the hundreds of promotional vehicles to follow, children had to apply their own decals to the Jack "Rabbit" Special if they wanted a Jack-in-the-Box version.

The Classic Nomad, produced in 1970 and 1971, became one of the brand's most remembered models. It featured custom vertically stacked quad headlights and an oversized sunroof. Although the brown version is the rarest of all Nomads (trading for over $200), this woman seems to be happy just sitting atop the realistically ribbed tailgate.

Tom Daniel designed fantasy model car kits for the Monogram company, and Mattel was already producing some of his designs when they purchased Monogram in 1971. This deal allowed Mattel to reproduce more of Daniel's now-classic cars. Pictured, from left to right: the Paddy Wagon, Red Baron, S'Cool Bus, Sand Crab, and Ice "T."

for the next few years, Larry Wood became synonymous with the Hot Wheels style and remains a part of the design team today.

1971

With Hot Wheels sales remaining brisk throughout 1970, Mattel made plans to offer even more new models for 1971. In fact, 1971 saw 35 new vehicles, more than in any previous year. Seven new Heavyweights trucks were added, as well as two new Spoilers, Snake and Mongoose rail dragsters, and new versions of the Snake and Mongoose funny cars. The Hot Wheels fantasy designs of Larry Wood, Howard Rees, Paul Tam, and Bob Lovejoy became even more prominent in the line with 12 new models. All of these were original creations with little or no recognizable resemblance to any real car. The designers also continued the tradition of "extreme customization" of real cars, creating six new models in this vein.

The extreme customs of 1971 included three vehicles by Wood: the Dodge Challenger-based double-engined Bye-Focal; the Grass Hopper; and the T-4-2, a Ford Model T with two front ends grafted together. Howard Rees designed the Cockney Cab, a hot-rodded version of a classic British Austin taxi, and the Short Order, a radically reproportioned 1950s Ford pickup truck featuring an extended hood with an exposed metal engine and a dramatically shortened bed in the back. Paul Tam created the Evil Weevil, a Volkswagen Beetle with two engines—one in the back and one in the front.

Larry Wood, Mattel's most famous Hot Wheels designer, created the Mutt Mobile for the 1971 lineup. A fantasy dog-catcher truck, its cargo section featured a swing-open cage door and two molded plastic dogs inside. According to Wood, "Mattel often finds out about new models to make from the auto makers themselves." The Mutt Mobile was clearly straight out of Wood's imagination.

Of the dozen original Hot Wheels fantasy designs introduced in 1971, the most remembered is the Mutt Mobile. Ostensibly a dog catcher's truck, the Mutt Mobile was designed by Larry Wood with a white plastic roof that incorporated a Model T–style overhanging roof for the driver as well as an enclosed rear section housing two plastic dogs and featuring an opening cage door. Mattel honored this design in 1994 by reissuing it as part of its Vintage Collection. Another notable Wood design was the Special Delivery, which used a U.S. mailbox—the blue ones seen on street corners—as the basis for a double-engined hot rod car. The idea of building toy cars around an object such as a mailbox resurfaced later with the Radio Flyer Wagon in 1996 and the Express Lane (grocery cart) and Hot Seat (toilet), both from 1998.

One of the most sought-after Hot Wheels cars, the 1971 Olds 442 is expensive today because of a limited-production run and its appealing realism. Collectors often pay more than $500 for a pristine red version like this one.

The idea of naming Hot Wheels cars with puns and wordplay became an established part of the Hot Wheels brand. (The trend started in 1969 with the Splittin' Image, an Ira Gilford fantasy car featuring twin bubble-topped passenger compartments.) By 1971 the idea was firmly entrenched and even expected of Hot Wheels toys. Evil Weevil, for example, was based on a Volkswagen Beetle (a weevil is a type of beetle). Rocket-Bye-Baby, a fantasy car with a metal rocket attached to the roof, played off of the old children's song "Rock-A-Bye, Baby." Six Shooter, a model with six wheels, referred to a pistol and the car's six wheels (something unimaginable in today's anti-gun climate). Strip Teaser used it's double entendre of the drag strip for an amusing play on words. T-4-2 played with the Ford Model T name, and cleverly indicated that this vehicle was built for two people (going in opposite directions). The joke became clear when its two front ends were noticed. This device is one that Mattel still employs today with cars like the Tee'd Off, a hot-rodded golf cart; Semi-Fast, a racing truck cab; and the Screamin' Hauler concept car.

In 1971 there were already enough "mostly stock" vehicles in the Hot Wheels mix to warrant

The 1971 Classic Cord (really a late-1930s Cord 812 convertible) became an instant favorite with collectors. Designer Larry Wood kept the customizing to a minimum, with the most prominent alteration being a blown engine sticking through the opening hood. When I asked author and collector Michael Strauss (*Tomart's Price Guide to Hot Wheels*) what his favorite Hot Wheels cars were, this was the first car he mentioned.

only three new ones: the AMX/2, Classic Cord, and Olds 442. Of course, they all featured the classic Hot Wheels mags and redline tires, and the Cord even had a blower unit sticking from a hole cut into its opening hood, but otherwise these three cars were pretty much box stock. The AMX/2 was based on a real mid-engined (non-working) experimental car debuted in 1969 by American Motors, the Cord replicated the Classic 1937 "coffin nose" 812 convertible, and the 442 was based on the 1970 Oldsmobile Cutlass 442, used that year to pace the Indianapolis 500. Popular with collectors, the Cord's curvy pontoon fenders were particularly well suited to showing off the nuances of Mattel's glimmering Spectraflame paint. The 442 ranks high in popularity as well, but prices for it today run higher than the Cord reportedly due to a shorter production run and because it was the only realistic model of a contemporary car issued in 1971.

The 1971 Heavyweights paired mostly existing diecast components like truck cabs and trailer chassis with newly tooled plastic beds and trailer bodies to create six new vehicles: the Fuel Tanker, Racer Rig, Scooper, Snorkel, Team Trailer, and Waste Wagon. The S'Cool Bus, introduced in 1971, was the only Heavyweights model that did not follow the futuristic look of the other vehicles. It wasn't even a working truck. Rather, the Tom Daniel–designed S'Cool Bus was a double-engined school funny car dragster, complete with flip-up body.

The Snake and Mongoose funny cars were re-colored—white and blue respectively—to reflect

Previous Page: Mattel's sponsorship of Tom "The Mongoose" McEwen and Don "The Snake" Prudhomme continued in 1971 with their real-life rail dragsters. The beautifully modeled miniatures of these cars featured weighted "wheelie wheels" in the back, which made the toys flip up in the front, just like the real racers. These two miniatures were always sold together, either in a blisterpack or track set.

changes made to the real racers. Mattel also sponsored Don Prudhomme's and Tom McEwen's rail dragsters, and made miniatures of both. The Hot Wheels versions featured cleverly designed weighted wheelie-wheel assemblies that tipped the front of the car up as it raced down the track. The Snake and Mongoose rail dragsters were found only in a dual blisterpack (featuring both cars) or the Wild Wheelie track set.

1972

While 1971 was a banner year for new models, the market seemed to have finally reached its saturation point for Hot Wheels vehicles. The Heavyweights and Spoilers lines were discontinued for 1972, but a few other models soldiered on. Those cars and only seven new castings carried the Hot Wheels line through 1972. Mattel discontinued the metal collector buttons, packaged with the cars since the beginning. This would also be the last year for the now-familiar Spectraflame paint. In addition, cars would no longer be made in California; all production moved to Hong Kong where labor was cheaper.

While the outlook seemed bleak, at least the new castings for 1972 were well executed. For example, the Ferrari 512S was an accurate model of a Pininfarina design study from 1969. The Pininfarina concept car's chassis and drivetrain were based on the race-winning Ferrari 512S. Like the original show car, the model's windshield tilted forward to allow access to the cockpit and the engine cover flipped backward to expose the Ferrari 12-cylinder engine. The Mercedes-Benz C-111 was another real car—built by Mercedes to showcase the possibilities of the Wankel engine. The Hot Wheels model featured opening gullwing doors, as in the actual vehicle.

Mattel introduced two new Snake and Mongoose dragsters—this time the contemporary rear-engined, wedge-bodied style. The dragsters were available in a racing set, and, for the first time, they were available on separate blistercards.

Paul Tam created a bizarre but beautifully rendered model of a six-wheeled AMC Gremlin called Open Fire. The extra pair of wheels rode under a giant, exposed metal engine. Other than the engine, extra wheels, and elongated hood, Open Fire retains many accurate styling details of AMC's quirky 1970s econocar.

Mattel introduced only seven new castings for 1972. The Ferrari 512S was perhaps the most beautiful. Replicating a full-size design study by Pininfarina, the real 1969 concept car was based on the chassis and drivetrain of Ferrari's 512S racing car.

Larry Wood created another one of his signature fantasy cars, Side Kick. Pull on the plastic tailpipes and the driver's seat slides out of the body horizontally. He also created Funny Money, a Funny Car with the body of an armored truck. Side Kick and Funny Money, as well as Open Fire and the Snake and Mongoose dragsters, were only issued in 1972.

The first era in Hot Wheels history, the Spectraflame years, ended in 1972. Spectraflame paint, in its original formula, would never be used again. From 1968 to 1972, Mattel introduced classic vehicles that remain in the Hot Wheels line even today: the Nomad, '67 Camaro, and Mantis among them.

With the Mongoose and Snake funny cars and rail dragsters, Mattel encouraged the growing sport of organized drag racing. The five-year period from 1968 to 1972 proved to be a wild ride, and Mattel responded swiftly and deftly to the incredible demand for its product.

Hot Wheels cars introduced the world's children to American-style vehicles, specifically California custom cars and fantasy creations that originated in Mattel's design department. But in 1972 it was time for Mattel to regroup and offer children a fresh take on Hot Wheels cars. Plans were under way to offer something completely different the following year.

Starting with the Custom AMX in 1969, Mattel designers exhibited a fondness for American Motors products which lasted for several years. This 1972 Open Fire is an accurate model of the quirky Gremlin, except, of course, for its extra set of wheels and enormous exposed engine.

1973–1977: Enamels, Flying Colors, and the End of Redlines

1973

The second era of Hot Wheels production began in 1973. Gone was the excitement of numerous exuberant yearly model introductions, as well as the trademark glimmering Spectraflame paint. Although hard to imagine today, Hot Wheels production outweighed sales in 1972. Mattel had to do something drastic, while keeping costs to a minimum for the new model year. The answer was paint.

Mattel replaced the 17 Spectraflame shades with 11 colors of opaque lacquer, called "enamels" by many collectors. Contrary to popular belief that Spectraflame colors were more expensive to produce, in fact the opposite was true. The Spectraflame cars used only one coat of tinted transparent lacquer. The new enamel-painted cars used two coats of lacquer: first a primer, then the colored topcoat. Mattel intended the new paint colors to recharge the brand; they had the added benefit of hiding the inherent imperfections and corrosive quality of diecast metal castings. While most of the colors were nonmetallic, two of them, fluorescent lime and fluorescent pink, featured very fine metallic flakes, which added a shimmering pearlescent quality to a vehicle's body. As with the cars in the Spectraflame era, Mattel painted each car in the 1973 line in most of the 11 new enamel colors.

In addition to the new paint, the appearance of the classic redline wheels also began to change. More and more models featured a new wheel that exposed the axle in the center.

For 1973, Mattel issued only three all-new castings: the Double Header, Superfine Turbine, and Sweet 16. The Double Header, a chunky fantasy vehicle designed by Paul Tam and Larry Wood, featured two turbine-like engines mounted on each side of the car. Mattel produced the model for only one year. The Superfine Turbine, also designed by Wood, mated a huge metal turbine engine with a Ford Model T-like body. It too lasted for only a year. Paul Tam loosely based the only other new model, Sweet 16, on a 1920s vintage Mercedes roadster. In classic Hot Wheels style, he substituted a 16-cylinder engine for the real car's straight six.

The Police Cruiser was a modified casting based on the Oldsmobile 442 of 1971. While the Cruiser's chassis remained the same, sirens and a mounting hole for the red plastic emergency light were added to the body.

This 1973 Superfine Turbine, designed by Larry Wood, was only in the Hot Wheels line for one year. Consequently, it often sells today for more than $400.

Numerous older castings were brought into the 1973 lineup with new names. The Classic Nomad became Alive '55, Sand Crab was now Dune Daddy, Mutt Mobile was Odd Job, and the Demon became Prowler, to name a few. American Motors must have been pleased to have its handsome AMX/2 concept car renamed Xploder.

Further proof of Mattel's cost-saving mode was the use of the same body casting—the Barracuda—for both new versions of the Snake and Mongoose funny cars. (Tom "The Mongoose" McEwen drove a Plymouth Duster.) Both the Snake and the Mongoose also lost their window glass for 1973. Even though these models were diluted versions of the originals, they were only issued for one year, making them scarce and pricey today.

A few cars survived the transition with their original names intact. The Ferrari 312P, Ice "T,"

Perhaps the most interesting of the three 1973 castings was the Sweet 16. It paired a vintage Mercedes body with a miniature diecast 16-cylinder engine.

Mercedes-Benz C-111 and 280SL, Paddy Wagon, Porsche 917, and Red Baron all soldiered on. If they didn't already wear enamel paint (like the Paddy Wagon and Ice "T"), they did for 1973.

Although Mattel's first promotional Hot Wheels car—the Jack-in-the-Box Jack "Rabbit" Special—was offered regionally in 1970, the company's first national project was with Shell Oil. The promotion featured 10 existing cars: Bugeye, Ferrari 512S, Jet Threat, Peepin' Bomb, Rocket-Bye-Baby, Short Order, Strip Teaser, Swingin' Wing (without the wing!), Splittin' Image, and TwinMill. Fill up your tank and get a free Hot Wheels car! According to collector Lance Joseph, an additional enamel color was used on some of the Shell promo cars. You won't find this medium-green metallic on cars in the regular Hot Wheels line, but you can see a sample of it in the enamel color chart.

While any mention of the 1973 Hot Wheels cars generates great excitement among collectors today, that year was crucial to the survival of the brand. Even with the paucity of new models, the switch from Spectraflame paint to opaque enamel colors seemed to work. By using mostly existing castings, simply re-colored, the Hot Wheels line began to recover.

1974

Mattel had more ambitious plans for the 1974 model year. Along with the introduction of seven new castings, the company applied the painting technique known as tampo to these and all other vehicles in the Hot Wheels line. Mattel called the newly decorated Hot Wheels cars "Flying Colors," and to promote them the new name was added to the Hot Wheels blisterpack.

The 1973 Hot Wheels models launched the new enamel colors—pristine and without decoration. In 1974, the idea of embellishing the cars with multicolored paint decorations was so tempting that no vehicle remained untouched. Designers added flames to the Rodger Dodger and Sir Rodney roadster, racing number graphics to the Heavy Chevy and Baja Bruiser; even flowers and peace signs appeared on the Funny Money armored truck. Because the hues of

"I started collecting Hot Wheels because I got them free! Shell Oil (gas stations) gave them away when I was in my 20s."
—Michael Thomas Strauss, collector and author of **Tomart's Price Guide to Hot Wheels**

these new graphics were designed to coordinate with only one or two body colors, the old system of painting a car in a selection of enamel colors was dead. It was cost prohibitive to design new tampo color schemes that would work with each body color. However, Mattel occasionally painted a few cars in a limited run of a different body color. This happened for a variety of reasons, the most common being that the original color ran out at the factory and an alternate was substituted. Since the tampo colors did not change, Mattel had to make sure that the new body color coordinated. These short-run variations are highly sought after today, often selling for 10 times the price of their common cousin. A few examples of these rare paint colors are the yellow version of the normally orange Baja Bruiser, the light-green version of the yellow Heavy Chevy, and the blue version of the common plum-colored Rodger Dodger.

In addition to the new tampo decorations, the Hot Wheels line added seven new vehicles. Although the rarest is the yellow Road King truck, a dump truck found only in the Mountain Mining Set, some of the more interesting cars were the Breakaway Bucket, an El Camino-style vehicle with a Pontiac Grand Am front, the Sir Rodney Roadster, a hot-rodded version of the Lotus Super 7, and the Baja Bruiser, a roll-cage-protected 1956 Ford pickup truck designed for off-road racing.

A few older models reappeared too. The Carabo (1970), Funny Money (1972), and Heavy Chevy (1970)

The 1974 Breakaway Bucket was a curious El Camino-like hybrid with a Pontiac Grand Am front and futuristic, one-piece wraparound windshield. Models this year were sold on new blistercards marked "Flying Colors." This referred to the colorful new tampo designs printed on their bodies. The Breakaway Bucket was made only in the blue and orange color variation pictured here.

In 1974, Mattel stopped issuing cars in a variety of colors. Many models now came in only one color, but occasionally a limited run in an alternate color would appear. This is what happened with the Sir Rodney Roadster, a custom sports car loosely based on the Lotus Super Seven. Mattel originally issued the car in yellow. The more scarce green version came later in the year.

all returned with new decoration but with their original names intact. Other older vehicles returned with new names. The Rash 1 was formerly the Brabham-Repco F1 (1969), Top Eliminator was the Snake Funny Car (1970-1973), Winnipeg was the Chapparal 2G (1969), and the Volkswagen was almost identical to the Custom Volkswagen from 1968. Although Mattel started this renaming trend with some of its models a year earlier, the practice

During its first two years of production, 1974 and 1975, the Baja Bruiser featured a metal chassis. After that, Mattel switched to "chromed" plastic. This customized 1956 Ford pickup remained in the line through the early 1980s.

The first Hot Wheels toy fair vehicle appeared in 1975. Mattel used their new Super Van casting and applied tampo designs promoting the still-new Flying Colors theme.

became entrenched by 1974 and would be employed often over the next 25 years, adding to the collector's confusion today.

1975

Ultimately, the tampo-painted cars and the recoloring of older castings worked. Sales were up and Mattel made plans to expand the Hot Wheels line for 1975. Over 20 new models were introduced in 1975, the most since the line's peak of 35 additions in 1971. For the first time, Mattel experimented with motorcycles and military vehicles. As a cost-cutting measure, the chassis on some cars were now made from plastic. This had the added benefit of making some vehicles run faster on Hot Wheels track. Another clever trick, according to collector Lance Joseph, was to use the same "chromed"-plastic chassis of a Dodge truck on six new vehicles: the Backwoods Bomb (camper), Emergency Squad, Ranger Rig, Super Van, Paramedic, and Ramblin' Wrecker.

Of the 23 new models, only two were classic Hot Wheels fantasy vehicles—the Large Charge racer and the Sand Drifter dune buggy. All of the other cars, if not totally stock, were based in some way on a real vehicle. In addition to typical Hot

Mattel introduced two motorcycles into the Hot Wheels line in 1975: the Motocross 1 and the Street Eater. Their diecast metal chassis and engine components were identical; only the plastic seat and fuel tank assemblies differed. Notable because they were the first motorcycles in the Hot Wheels line, Mattel struck motorcycle gold 22 years later with the immensely popular Scorchin' Scooter.

Wheels models such as a Porsche 911, Vega Funny Car, and McLaren racer (called American Victory) Mattel made a completely stock version—other than the tampo graphics—of the newly introduced Chevy Monza 2+2.

The Mighty Maverick reappeared, as well as the popular Olds 442, this time in red as the Chief's Special fire chief car. Mattel's affinity for AMC products became clear with the release of the Gremlin Grinder. (The first Gremlin was the six-wheeled Open Fire in 1972.) The Gremlin Grinder featured a monster exposed metal engine and rode on four wheels, not six. The Gremlin appeared again, in dirt track form, in 1979, and even a Pacer Wagon made an appearance in 1978.

For the first time, the Hot Wheels line also included two stock car racers: a Monte Carlo and a Torino. Both cars featured generic decoration instead of authentic sponsor graphics, which didn't happen in a big way until 1992 with the introduction of Pro Circuit vehicles. In fact, stock cars played a relatively minor role in the Hot Wheels lineup until 1997, when Mattel began sponsoring Kyle Petty's #44 Pontiac, and simultaneously began producing entire fleets of authentically painted NASCAR Monte Carlos, Thunderbirds, and Grand Prix.

The 1975 Ranger Rig casting is still in production today, albeit with a new paint scheme and under the name Rescue Ranger. To save costs, Mattel cleverly used the exact same Dodge chassis for five other trucks that year: the Backwoods Bomb (camper), Emergency Squad, Super Van, Paramedic, and Ramblin' Wrecker.

"There is something more tangible when you hold a 30-year-old car in your hand, versus a car stuck in the blister. You wonder about the history behind the car. Who owned it? Where are they now?"
—*Neal Giordano, collector and president of the North Carolina Hot Wheels Association*

Here is another Hot Wheels car that can still be found on the peg today—the Porsche 911. The earliest version, shown here, features deep yellow paint and the Porsche name molded crisply between the taillights.

Numerous early promotional Hot Wheels cars were made for the Herfy's restaurant chain. The three pictured here, all from 1975, are the Chief's Special (Olds 442), Super Van, and Warpath (AMX/2).

1976

Now in its third year, Flying Colors continued as the predominant theme in the basic Hot Wheels line. The biggest news for 1976 was a promotional series called Super Chromes. Mattel took 18 vehicles—6 new ones and 12 existing models—and "chrome-plated" them like the old Club Kit cars of 1970–1971. Unlike the old club cars, which were "chrome" with two black stripes running over the length of the car, the new Super Chromes wore colorful tampo designs often exactly the same as the "non-chrome" car in the standard Flying Colors line. The six new cars—Neet Streeter, Poison Pinto, Rock Buster, TwinMill II, Corvette Stingray, and Formula 5000—came in sets only. The other 12 cars came individually blisterpacked.

In honor of America's bicentennial, Mattel painted four of its new basic line vehicles with red, white, and blue graphics. The American Tipper, a dump truck, and the American Hauler, a moving van, featured heavy diecast chassis and cabs mated to white plastic beds or boxes decorated with red and blue tampo stampings simulating the American flag. The Formula 5000 was an F1-style racer with "76" graphics. The Neet Streeter was a new casting—unfortunately without the working rumble seat—of 1969's Classic '36 Ford Coupe. Its homage to the bicentennial was a little less obvious: the car was painted light blue and wore red, white, and blue graphics stating, "Oldie but a Goodie."

For 1976, Mattel also produced four new military vehicles—the Gun Bucket, Aw Shoot, Khaki Kooler, and Staff Car—to join two that were launched the previous year. The Gun Bucket was resurrected in 1985 as the Tank Gunner and in 1996 (with gun removed) as the Swingfire. The Khaki Kooler was really just a paint variation of the Super

For 1976, Mattel introduced a line of 18 vehicles called Super Chromes. Each was "chrome plated" and featured colorful tampo decoration. The Corvette Stingray was a new model for 1976, and came as a Super Chromes model, shown here, or painted red.

To celebrate America's bicentennial, Mattel painted four new castings with red, white, and blue color schemes. One of these was the American Tipper dump truck. Its roomy bed was perfect for hauling away all of the mannequins used in the photo shoot for this book.

The 1976 Poison Pinto. Did Mattel know something that Ford didn't?

Van introduced a year earlier, and the Staff Car was another color variation, this time of the Maxi Taxi, which itself was a diluted version of the Olds 442 first introduced in 1971.

Of all the new castings for 1976, the contemporary Corvette Stingray became the most successful for Mattel over the years. More than 40 variations have been produced, including the original Super Chromes and red enamel versions, a racing variation in 1985, a gold "chrome" version produced for Hot Wheels cars' 20th anniversary, a Gleam Team version in textured green chrome in 1992, and a Real Riders version in 1995.

1977

In 1977 Mattel discontinued the trademark redline tires. Considering that raised white-letter tires replaced redlines on real cars in the early 1970s, redline tires were a strange relic for children in 1977 who didn't remember the real thing.

All models in 1977 were produced first with redline tires, then later in the year with blackwalls. Mattel used redlines in very limited quantities on some 1977 models—the GMC Motorhome, Show Hoss II, and T-Totaller, to name a few. Values for those cars can be 10 to 20 times greater than for the same car fitted with blackwall tires.

"I think collectors should always collect for fun. Don't go into collecting to make money."
—*Michael Thomas Strauss, collector and author of* **Tomart's Price Guide to Hot Wheels**

The '57 Chevy, first introduced in 1977, has remained in almost continuous production since its debut. Early models, such as this one, featured a traditional (fixed) hood. From 1984 on, most '57 Chevys had a giant, exposed metal engine.

A perennial favorite, the '57 Chevy was introduced in 1977 and has remained constantly in the line. From the original red-and-yellow version with redlines to later examples featuring Real Riders, Ultra Hot, Hot Ones, and contemporary five-spoke wheels, the '57 Chevy has survived over 75 variations.

Other new models destined to reappear more than 20 years later were the '31 Doozie, Fire-Eater (fire truck), GMC Motorhome, and Second Wind, a not-so-subtle copy of cartoon character Speed Racer's Mach 5. The year 1977 also saw the introduction of the first of three Nissan Z cars. The Z Whiz featured Datsun's first-generation Z car body style. Later versions came in 1985 and 1990.

The only new Hot Wheels fantasy vehicle released in 1977 was the Odd Rod. At first glance it seemed like a typical rear-engined dragster. A closer look revealed its clear body section in the front—the metal chassis was visible through it—and a seat for the driver and passenger. Odd indeed. Odder still that Mattel lifted the name Odd Rod from the popular 1969 Odd Rods trading cards from the DonRuss Company, which featured caricatures of grotesquely distorted humans or monsters usually driving some kind of wildly customized car.

We remember 1977 as the end of the long reign of the Hot Wheels redline. The wheel that was such a big part of the success of Hot Wheels cars had fulfilled its purpose. In the beginning it made Hot Wheels cars hip, trendy, and modern. But by 1977, red-stripe tires were out of fashion, and Mattel wisely decided to retire them.

Early versions (1977–1978) of the GMC Motorhome featured a metal chassis while the later variations switched to "chrome-plated" plastic. Find the redline version of this model and it could be worth more than $500 to some collectors.

Like the Baja Bruiser from 1974, Mattel based the '56 Hi-Tail Hauler on a 1956 Ford pickup truck. But the "Hauler" was designed for more traditional duties instead of racing. It featured two plastic motorcycles molded into the bed.

The Odd Rod, which featured quirky fantasy design cues like older Hot Wheels models, was an anomaly by 1977. Its Model T passenger compartment and clear plastic nose demonstrated classic Hot Wheels creativity, a direction that seemed to have changed in favor of more reality-based vehicles.

1978–1981: Entering the Second Decade

1978

From the first year of production, Mattel made a large part of the Hot Wheels line in Hong Kong, where labor certainly was cheaper. Fortunately, quality was equal to that of the cars made in California. To meet the growing demand for its product, and to help keep costs down, Mattel opened a new plant in Malaysia in 1982. The period from 1978 to 1981 represents the last era where vehicles were produced exclusively in Hong Kong.

The big news for 1978 was that every vehicle featured blackwall tires. Redlines were gone forever from the basic line, only to be resurrected periodically on commemorative models or special promotional vehicles. Mattel also placed each of its 1978 vehicles into one of seven thematic groups. Speedway Specials featured sports or racing cars and trucks; Super Streeters included traditional, stock versions of cars; Oldies But Goodies celebrated vintage cars; The Heavies featured working or commercial vehicles like trucks, motorhomes, and taxis; Drag Strippers grouped funny cars, dragsters, and other racers together; Rescue Team featured emergency vehicles; and Classy Customs were Mattel's signature fantasy vehicles. The company designed a new blistercard for each group, and offered kids a mail-away embroidered patch unique to each series.

Of the dozen new castings introduced in 1978, a few were destined to lead long lives in the Hot Wheels lineup. The '57 T-Bird debuted in white and included the classic porthole-windowed hardtop found on the real first-generation Thunderbirds. That feature soon disappeared from the casting, but the model remained in the line for more than 20 years. Within two decades Mattel produced over 45 versions of Ford's timeless roadster.

Also in 1978, Mattel released the Hot Bird, a contemporary Pontiac Firebird Trans Am. A car made famous in its day by the *Smokey and the Bandit* films, the black Hot Wheels version featured a period T-top and a Firebird emblem on the hood. Later variations—25 in all—featured stock versions in brown, blue, silver, and gold, as well as custom-painted models in multicolored metalflake and gold "chrome."

Three other castings enjoyed a long life in the Hot Wheels line. The Baja Breaker, a four-wheel-drive Ford van, saw 15 variations, including its latest in 1997, noted for its purple body with yellow

---

The '57 T-Bird, introduced in 1978, featured a molded-on hardtop with porthole windows. This casting has remained in almost continuous production since its inception. It differed greatly from Mattel's original classic '57 T-Bird of 1969, which was a speedster-style, open-topped car.

Made famous by the *Smokey and the Bandit* movie a year earlier, Mattel introduced a black Pontiac Trans Am in 1978. They called it the Hot Bird and it remained in the line, in one color or another, for almost 20 years.

polka-dot decoration. The 1978 Highway Patrol, a Dodge-like police car, reappeared in 1979 as a fire chief car (Fire Chaser) and in 1982 as the Sheriff Patrol. Its most recent variation appeared in the Action Pack Police Force set of 1997. (Action Packs, introduced in 1997, usually paired two vehicles with molded plastic figures or accessories.)

And finally, the Race Bait 308—really a Ferrari 308 GTB—debuted in 1978 in classic Ferrari red and wearing oversized "308 GTB" graphics on the hood. The proportions of this model rank it as one of the all-time best Hot Wheels cars for casting accuracy. The Race Bait 308 captures the smoothly bulging fenders, pinched midsection, and seamless roofline of this classic Ferrari. The Race Bait 308 remained in production through the early 1980s, then reappeared in 1984 as the Quik Trik, in 1985 as the Street Beast, and in the late 1990s with its proper name, the Ferrari 308 GTB.

Mattel once again produced a Don Prudhomme "The Snake" Plymouth-bodied funny car, but this time it featured U.S. Army rather than Hot Wheels sponsorship, and the car was an Arrow instead of the discontinued Barracuda. No Mongoose model joined the new Plymouth Arrow Snake.

Mattel's fondness for AMC products resurfaced with the Packin' Pacer, a Pacer station wagon transformed into a rear-engined dragster. Other than the rear engine, this car was an accurate and realistic copy of a 1970s automotive icon.

Mattel added two fantasy vehicles to the lineup for 1978: Science Friction and Stagefright. A futuristic, hot-rodded police car, Science Friction featured a huge, rear-mounted "chromed-plastic" engine and orange plastic guns and lights. Stagefright, in the tradition of George Barris' Munster Coach and Tom Daniel's Red Baron, transformed an unmotorized object—in this case a stagecoach—into a hot rod.

Take away the gratuitous tampo printing on the 1978 Race Bait 308's hood and you find one of the most accurately cast Hot Wheels cars. The real Ferrari 308 featured fluid, undulating fenders, and a streamlined greenhouse integrated seamlessly into the overall body design. Mattel's model was right on the mark.

Here is the next piece of evidence of Mattel's fondness for AMC products—the 1978 Packin' Pacer. It features a monster "chrome-plated" engine in the back, but otherwise follows the stock lines of the often-maligned Pacer station wagon.

In 1979, Mattel entered into a licensing agreement with Marvel Comics and produced a number of vehicles featuring images of comic book characters. These cars were part of the Heroes series. Mattel also introduced Scene Machines in 1979. Each featured a clear plastic lens fitted into the vehicle's body that upon looking through revealed a printed comic book scene. Some Scene Machines featured Marvel characters. Pictured here are a Captain America Scene Machine and an Incredible Hulk Heroes vehicle, both from 1979, and a Silver Surfer Heroes car from 1981.

1979

A stable period for Hot Wheels cars, 1979 saw the introduction of 14 new castings. Mattel also launched two new series in 1979: Scene Machines and Heroes. Scene Machines featured a design whereby a child looked through a plastic magnifying lens fitted at one end of the vehicle and saw a picture of some related object inside. The Incredible Hulk van, for example, housed a printed picture of the cartoon character himself lunging toward the viewer. Heroes featured images of famous Marvel Comics characters such as Spider-Man, The Incredible Hulk, and Captain America. (Some Scene Machines also featured Marvel characters.) In the Heroes series, Mattel applied images of these comic book characters to numerous existing models. The Incredible Hulk ended up on the Spoiler Sport van, Thor on the Super Van, and Captain America on the Hot Bird (Firebird). Mattel made the only new casting for Spider-Man in the Heroes series. Painted black with a body cast to resemble an actual spider, this vehicle was the first biomorphically shaped Hot Wheels car. An entire fleet of animal-shaped vehicles appeared in 1986.

Other new castings for 1979 included the Bywayman and Auburn 852. The Bywayman, a Chevrolet 4x4 pickup truck, enjoyed continued popularity throughout its long history of over 45 variations (including snow plow duty as the Super Scraper, Pavement Pounder, and Power Plower) through the years. The Auburn 852, a famous boat-tailed speedster from the mid-1930s, displays outstanding realism, including metal bumpers and "chrome-plated" grille, headlights, and windshield frame. In 1996, Mattel used the Auburn as a Treasure Hunt car and included it in the American Classics three-car set. The

The only original casting created for the Heroes line was that of the Spider-Man car from 1979. Shaped like a spider and featuring bulging red windshield "eyes," this biomorphic vehicle predated an entire line of similar cars (called Speed Demons) introduced in 1986.

1998 Hot Wheels convention organizers also chose the Auburn as one of several unpainted Zamak cars to use as promotions for the event.

Mattel introduced four new fantasy cars for 1979: Bubble Gunner, Dumpin' A, Space Van, and Spacer Racer. None became Hot Wheels classics, and they remained in the line for only a few years.

Two foreign sports cars in stock trim appeared in 1979: Royal Flash (Lotus Esprit) and Upfront (Porsche) 924. Porsche introduced its affordable and popular front-engined 924 in 1976. Lotus introduced the Esprit the same year, and in 1977 it was prominently featured in the James Bond film *The Spy Who Loved Me*. Although Mattel introduced the miniatures three years after the real cars hit the streets, the designs were still fresh. Within a few years, the real Porsche 924 evolved into the 944 (using a similar body), which lasted through 1991. Amazingly, the real Lotus Esprit is still in production with few changes to its rakish Giugiaro-styled body.

Mattel introduced a new Tom McEwen "Mongoose" funny car for 1979 called Vetty Funny (a Corvette, of course), but like the Don Prudhomme funny car of a year earlier, this new racer was no longer sponsored by Hot Wheels cars. Three other racers debuted that year: Flat Out 442, Greased Gremlin, and Hare Splitter. While the Flat Out (Oldsmobile) 442 was made to resemble a stock car, it's hard to image any of General Motors' late 1970s "aeroback" cars competing in a race. The Greased Gremlin—yes, this was the third Gremlin-based Hot Wheels car—remained an accurate

In 1979, Mattel introduced the Auburn 852, long a favorite of collectors despite its plastic fenders. Accurate proportions, combined with its metal chassis and bumpers, make up for the abundance of plastic in the bodywork.

Exhibit number four (did I forget to mention the Gremlin Grinder in 1975?) of Mattel's obsession with AMC products—the 1979 Greased Gremlin. Real Gremlins ceased production the year before, but there were plenty of old ones left to use on dirt-track racing circuits. This realistic model of a now-vintage racer is an accurate time capsule of a popular short-track racing car.

Mattel introduced a new series in 1980 called Hi-Rakers. Each of the six vehicles featured a rear axle that could be ratcheted into varying degrees of rake. This 3-Window '34 Ford is posed in its highest position, as if waiting for a challenge from the nearest hot rod.

miniature of a Gremlin dirt track racer, and the Hare Splitter was a credible Volkswagen Golf rally car. Mattel even added roof-mounted lights and a spare tire for realism.

Finally, for 1979 Mattel offered a six-pack of "gold-chrome-plated" cars called Golden Machines. None were new castings; they derived from models introduced during the three previous years. The set included the Race Bait (Ferrari) 308, Jaguar XJS, Spoiler Sport (van), Z Whiz (Datsun), Hot Bird (Firebird), and Corvette Stingray. Today these models bring a premium, selling for more than $25 each.

1980

For 1980, Mattel dropped all seven theme groups it had launched in 1978. Heroes and Scene Machines continued, but no new models were added. Mattel introduced two completely new series, however: Hi-Rakers and Workhorses.

Hi-Rakers used a unique positionable rear axle assembly. Kids could pull the rear wheels out from the body to give the car varying degrees of the classic hot rod stance or "rake." In its fully retracted position the car sat normally. Mattel launched the series with six new castings: the 3-Window '34 (Ford), '40s

The new Workhorses series debuted in 1980 and included the Hiway Hauler, a short-box delivery truck featuring opening rear doors. Its wide, flat surfaces provided ample room for advertising logos and slogans and through the years it has probably seen more promotional versions than any other casting. Mattel replaced the Hiway Hauler in 1992 with a new version, and the tradition continued of using it as a promotional giveaway.

(Ford) Woodie, Dodge D-50 (pickup truck), Split Window '63 (Corvette), Turbo Wedge (concept racer), and the 'Vette Van. Three of these, the '34 Ford, '40s Woodie, and Split Window '63, can still be found in the line today.

The Workhorses featured (no surprise here) construction vehicles. Over the next few years, this series used 24 different castings. In its first year, the Workhorses included six models: a moving truck called the Highway Hauler, a Peterbilt cement mixer, and four pieces of Caterpillar construction equipment—a bulldozer, dump truck, forklift, and wheel loader. A licensing agreement allowed Mattel to print or mold the name Caterpillar onto each of these models. Mattel clearly meant for the Caterpillar toys to be played with outside in the dirt. The bulldozer featured flexible plastic treads instead of wheels. Mattel created a new tire for the dump truck and wheel loader; its knobby tread was better suited to miniature dirt roads than smooth plastic Hot Wheels track.

Of the other new models for 1980, the Greyhound MC-8 bus is notable for its heft. Besides the windows and wheels, the entire vehicle is diecast metal—even the seats. In addition, the Hot Wheels line offered a current generation Mustang—a year after Ford introduced the real car. Other than the Boss Hoss funny car version, Mattel never produced a Hot Wheels model of the underpowered and often maligned Mustang II, made from 1974 to 1978. Also in 1980, Mattel introduced a model of the ultra-luxury Stutz Blackhawk—a car favored in Hollywood for its flamboyant design and exclusivity. In reality, Stutz used the chassis and drivetrain from the mundane Pontiac Grand Prix, rebodied the car in Italy, and trimmed the interior in luxury materials. The Hot Wheels Stutz Blackhawk remains the only model in 1/64th scale of this rare and quirky car from the 1970s.

The Workhorses series of 1980 included several Caterpillar construction vehicles. These were heavy, mostly metal models that featured construction tires or treads. Pictured here, moving coffee through the mountains of Colombia, are the CAT Bulldozer and the CAT Dump Truck.

1981

With 12 new models, 1981 seemed like just another year in Mattel's steady production of the popular Hot Wheels cars. What the consumer didn't know was that Mattel was readying plans for its new plant in Malaysia.

In addition, Mattel introduced a handsome new wheel on some of its models. These cars were called the Hot Ones, and they rode on wheels with gold- "chrome-plated" hubs styled more like real wheel designs of the early 1980s. Thirty-four cars eventually became part of the Hot Ones series, and Mattel promoted their new wheel by featuring the Hot Ones name on a newly designed blistercard. Mattel mounted these new wheels on a thinner axle for better racing speed. Despite their gold color, the Hot Ones hub is one of the most realistic wheels ever made by Mattel. Some Hot Ones wheels were eventually made with "chrome" hubs. According to collector Michael Strauss, a few Hot Wheels cars were actually issued with these new wheels a year earlier—the Corvette Stingray, Porsche 911, and Packin' Pacer among them.

Other important new castings for 1981 include the '37 Bugatti, (Ford) Bronco 4-Wheeler, and Old Number 5 (fire engine). All have been reissued many times over the years in various color and wheel variations. Notable for its flashy two-tone paint, the Bugatti also features two black plastic spare tires mounted on the trunk. It was chosen as one of 12 Treasure Hunt vehicles in 1996. Of the Bronco's 25 variations, two of the most interesting are the red 1982 version fitted with Real Riders wheels and the white 1991 Ecolab Pest Control promotional giveaway that featured a tall camper shell in the back. Old Number 5, an antique Ahrens Fox fire pumper truck, left the basic line in 1997 to be used as a Holiday Hot Wheels vehicle. Mattel fitted Pro Circuit Indy (racer) wheels, plated the truck's body in red or silver "chrome", and added three tiny plastic elves bearing gifts and a Christmas tree.

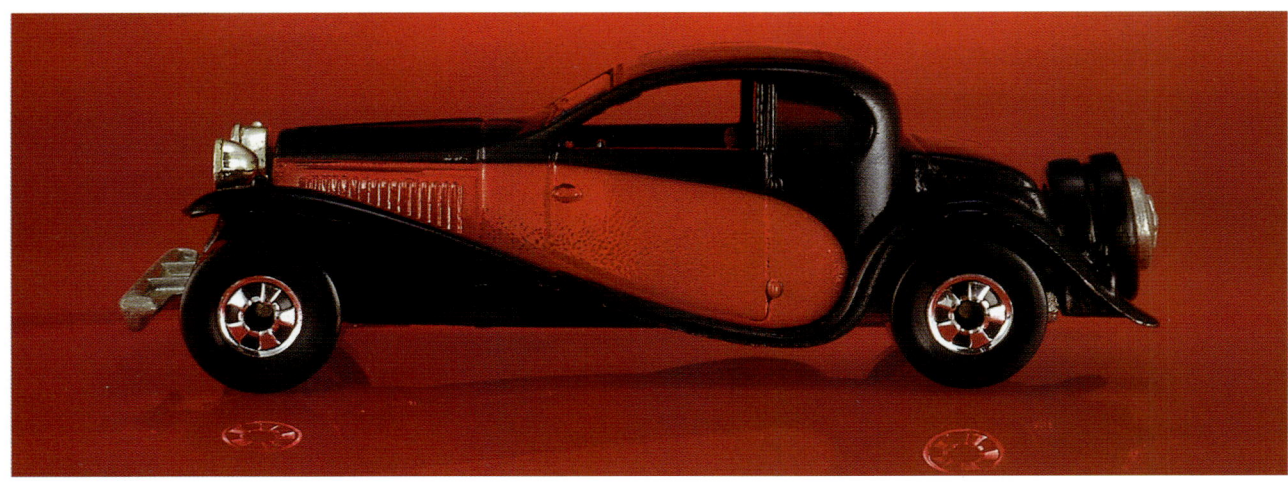

This '37 Bugatti from 1981 is perhaps the most handsome version of Mattel's elegant model. The black plastic fenders can be overlooked since they almost seamlessly blend with the black-painted diecast body.

Introduced in 1981, the Dixie Challenger was an obvious homage to the "General Lee," a 1969 Dodge Charger featured in *The Dukes of Hazzard* television series. No matter that the Hot Wheels version was a Dodge Challenger; it was painted the same bright orange and featured a Confederate battle flag on its roof.

A group of short-lived models also appeared in 1981. The hefty Airport Rescue fire truck was almost 3-1/2 inches long (most Hot Wheels cars ranged from 2-3/4 to 3 inches) and featured a diecast chassis and body and eight wheels. The Dixie (Dodge) Challenger, an obvious homage to the "General Lee" Dodge Charger from *The Dukes of Hazzard* television series, proudly wore an image of the Confederate battle flag on its roof, a concept that is hard to imagine today. And finally, Mattel chose two everyday American cars to reproduce: the Chevy Citation and the Dodge Omni 024. True, the miniature Citation was Chevrolet's "performance" version X/11 and the Omni was the sporty 024 coupe, but ultimately these were typical family cars and odd choices to be reproduced as Hot Wheels cars. This fact, combined with their accurate castings, makes them two of this author's favorite models from the period.

Another Hot Wheels model with a seemingly unlimited lifespan, the 1981 Bronco 4-Wheeler is still made today. This black version with red, yellow, and orange tampo was the first. Even better looking is the red Real Riders version from 1982. If one can be found, be prepared to spend about $100 for it.

65

1982–1988: Approaching 20 Years of Production

1982

In 1982 Mattel moved some of its production to a new facility in Malaysia. By 1987, all Hot Wheels models would be made there. The first new models to come from the Malaysian facility were three vehicles based on the *Megaforce* movie: the Battle Tank (a copy of the Tough Customer tank from 1975), and two versions of the Megadestroyer, an armored off-road assault vehicle. Because of the movie's dismal performance, Mattel abruptly ended production of these vehicles, making them hard to find today.

The McDonald's restaurant chain first used Hot Wheels cars as a promotion in 1982. Twenty-four different vehicles were available that year, including the Firebird funny car, Sheriff Patrol, and Jeep CJ-7. Giving away Hot Wheels cars has become a tradition at McDonald's, which still periodically offers Hot Wheels cars in their Happy Meals for kids. Today, however, the cars are designed especially for McDonald's. To save money, the new McDonald's cars use more plastic parts and fewer components.

New castings in the regular Hot Wheels line for 1982 included three vintage cars, which Mattel continued to reissue for many years: the '35 Classic Caddy, (1937) Mercedes 540K, and '55 Chevy. The '35 Cadillac, despite its Band-Aid-tan color, is one of the most beautiful and accurately proportioned classic cars that Mattel ever made. Despite its plastic fenders, the Cadillac's diecast metal body and chassis made it a heavy car. Details such as a "chrome-plated" grille and headlights and open driver's compartment added to the car's realism. Mattel's most recent release of the Cadillac featured a purple and black body with "chrome" lace wheels. The Mercedes 540K, the elegant and exclusive roadster from the late 1930s, was also accurately reproduced by Mattel. The model's flowing fenders, removable convertible top, and exposed metal exhaust pipes captured the allure of this exotic roadster. Mattel selected both the Cadillac and the Mercedes as Treasure Hunt cars in 1995 and 1999, respectively.

The '55 Chevy suffered in the area of realism. Mattel never fitted it with an interior, and the exposed side pipes and rear traction bars met under the doors in an awkward juxtaposition. Casting details are sketchy at best, and later models suffered the final insult of a plastic chassis. Even so,

---

What is it with Mattel and plastic fenders on their vintage cars? Luckily, it's easy to overlook them on this beautifully cast '35 Classic Caddy from 1982. This popular model remains in the line today.

In 1982, McDonald's first gave away Hot Wheels cars with their children's meals. Twenty-four regular line vehicles were the freebies. The tradition has continued, although the cars have become less detailed than regular Hot Wheels cars. They are now produced exclusively for McDonald's; fewer parts and more plastic mean lower production costs. Occasionally, a real beauty appears, like this car from a 1999 Happy Meal. For those who couldn't afford a $35 Boyd Coddington car from the Hot Wheels Custom Rods series, this model has many of the same styling cues as the sleek CadZZilla.

One of Mattel's periodic experiments with plastic-bodied vehicles is exemplified by the 1982 Rapid Transit. Its diecast metal chassis and seats made it weighty like other Hot Wheels models, and its body accurately replicated a contemporary city bus.

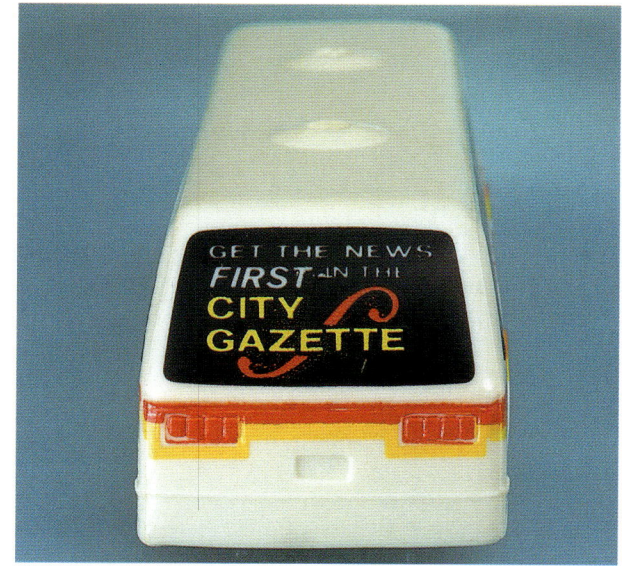

This is one of the author's favorite Hot Wheels cars—the (1982 Dodge) Aries wagon, complete with faux woodgrain trim on the sides. It falls completely outside of traditional Hot Wheels model choices. "Yeah, I think I'll drag race it against the Cadillac Seville," another curious Hot Wheels model from 1982.

Mattel used the '55 Chevy in more than 20 variations, most recently as a Cop Rods version made for K•B Toys in 1999.

Also destined for extended service in the Hot Wheels line were the Camaro Z-28 (with almost 40 variations since 1982) and the (Porsche) P-928. New variations of both appeared as recently as 1999. In 1982, Mattel also introduced the Mercedes 380 SEL, an authentic street version of a large Mercedes-Benz sedan. In a rare move, Mattel molded a dog—Matchbox style—into the back seat. With 33 variations since the original gray and black version, Mattel retired the 380 SEL in 1999. Its last variation was painted purple and was featured in a series called "Final Run" in which models of the past are retired.

Mattel made several intriguing model choices for 1982, among them the (Dodge) Aries Wagon, complete with tampo-painted faux wood on the sides, the ill-fated "bustle-back" Cadillac Seville in two-tone silver and magenta, a contemporary Peugeot 505 sedan, and the Front Runnin' Fairmont, an unlikely stock car based on the soon-to-be-discontinued (1983 was its last year) Ford Fairmont Futura Coupe.

A new Don Prudhomme "Snake" funny car debuted, this time with Pepsi sponsorship and based on the Snake's old Army funny car casting of 1978. As in 1978, no Mongoose funny car joined the Snake.

Of final note is the Sunagon, Volkswagen's Vanagon camper, which Mattel painted in authentic orange and tan and outfitted with a pop-up camper top. This casting, although not used since the late 1980s, remains one of Mattel's most realistic models of any vehicle.

Someone in the Hot Wheels design department was on a realism kick in 1982. The Sunagon, a Volkswagen Vanagon, is as accurate and realistic as any Matchbox car could ever hope to be. It featured authentic orange and tan two-tone paint and a pop-up plastic camper top.

1983

Mattel celebrated the 15th anniversary of Hot Wheels cars in 1983 with a three-car set featuring two cars from the basic line (specially painted) and a new casting of the 1967 Camaro, which, according to Mattel, was the first Hot Wheels car. Packaged with the three cars was a metal belt buckle molded with the Hot Wheels logo.

Mattel also launched a new series of vehicles called Real Riders. New packaging announced their special feature as, "Tires that look and feel like the real thing!" Mattel mounted a soft plastic tire to a rigid plastic hub. In most cases these wheels looked more realistic than the standard Hot Wheels issue, especially on four-wheel-drive vehicles and trucks. The Real Riders wheels were of a little larger scale than the standard wheel, so on cars they sometimes looked too large. Designed with raised white letter tires, they all featured a prominent "Goodyear" printed on their sidewalls. Appropriate on cars such as the Baja Bug, Bronco 4-Wheeler, and Bywayman

Mattel introduced a new series called Real Riders in 1983. Although they had already used the two-piece (plastic hub and soft tire) wheels on a few models before, they launched the official series this year. It eventually included 36 different castings. This Jeep Scrambler was one of the first models to appear.

(pickup truck), the wheels seemed a little strange on luxury cars such as the Mercedes 380 SEL and Cadillac Seville. Nevertheless, the series proved popular and cars fitted with Real Riders wheels command a premium price today.

According to collector Michael Strauss, Mattel used the Real Riders wheel on at least one car two years before the company launched the series. The A-OK (Ford Model A delivery truck) wore Real Riders wheels in 1981. This feature, combined with a short production run, made the A-OK a very scarce and valuable model. Mattel introduced at least five Real Riders cars in 1982, a year before it launched the official series. Although bringing nowhere near the price of a $400 A-OK, the '57 T-Bird, (Porsche) P-928, (1932 Ford) Street Rodder, Bronco 4-Wheeler, and Race Bait 308 (Ferrari) command prices from $30 to $100.

Over its four-year life, the Real Riders series eventually featured 36 vehicles—everything from classic cars such as the 3-Window '34 (Ford) and '40s (Ford) Woodie to contemporary sports cars such as the BMW M1 and (Porsche) P-928 to trucks such as the Dodge D-50 and Jeep CJ-7. Early models featured gray hubs; in subsequent years Mattel introduced white hubs as well.

Mattel also launched a smaller, short-lived series called Extras. Each of the seven vehicles included "extra" plastic parts that could be added to modify the car. For example, the '56 Hi-Tail Hauler (Ford pickup) included a camper top, the Upfront (Porsche) 924 had a ski rack, and the '31 Doozie featured a removable plastic top.

Also in 1983, Mattel decided to add production facilities in France for the European market, and Mexico for the Mexican market. Some of their

During the mid-1980s, Mattel produced a few Hot Wheels vehicles in France for the European market. Two of these cars were the Renault Le Car and Fiat Strada, both made in 1983. Unfortunately, these models were not sold in the United States and are difficult to find today.

vehicles, such as the Double Deck Bus, Fiat Ritmo, and Renault Le Car, were never released in the United States. In addition, paint variations different from those released on cars in the U. S. appeared in Mexico and France and today they bring a premium in the American collector market. This short-lived experiment in Mexican and French production ended in 1986, after only four years.

Of the 20 new Hot Wheels models introduced for 1983, several enjoyed continued popularity, in various versions, for more than 15 years. Mattel's first commemorative vehicle, the '67 Camaro, saw more than 35 different variations—everything from red enamel or metalflake lime in 1983, to a white and orange Treasure Hunt car in 1995, to a metalflake blue "Hot Wheels Race Team" version in 1998. The '80s Corvette and '80s Firebird each saw more than 20 variations. Of the two, the Corvette exhibited finer casting details, featuring an opening hood (on early versions), metal chassis, handsome gold Hot Ones wheels, and contrasting color seat inserts and luggage. The Firebird, while reasonably accurate in proportion, has an unusually wide bar between the T-tops and suffers from weak casting details like door and grille lines.

Mattel got it right with the Classic Cobra, an accurate model of Carroll Shelby's original Ford V-8-powered roadster of the 1960s. The first Hot Wheels version is painted in traditional navy blue with white stripes. Of the 40 subsequent variations, the metallic green Treasure Hunt Cobra of 1995, the metalflake blue Hot Wheels Racing Team version of 1998, and the Real Riders versions in navy, red, or "California Custom" white are collector favorites.

The year saw several other models that would last many years in the Hot Wheels line: the Beach Patrol (Chevrolet S-10 pickup), Peterbilt dump truck, (Ford) Rig Wrecker, Ford Stake Bed Truck, and Turbo Streak (Indy racer), all of which have had numerous and recent variations. Two of 1983's less common

One of the most popular Hot Wheels cars today, the Fat Fendered '40 started life in 1983 as the '40s Ford 2-Door, shown here. A large, heavy model with a diecast body and chassis, it was, in fact, a replica of a 1940 Ford.

Mattel introduced the Classic Cobra in 1983, another collector favorite. An accurate model of Carroll Shelby's Ford-powered 1960s sports car, the first Hot Wheels version, pictured here, featured standard blackwall tires. Later that year, Mattel fitted it with Real Riders wheels.

vehicles were actually some of the most handsome new releases. The Pontiac J-2000 was a realistic miniature of Pontiac's sporty and popular economy hatchback. It featured a sunroof, tasteful "J-2000" graphics, metal headlights cast as part of the chassis, and the same-sized front and rear wheels. Mattel only made one basic variation, in yellow, of the J-2000 for the U.S. market.

The other vehicle, a Jeep Scrambler, was based on a real Jeep that rode on a stretched CJ-5 chassis, producing a large open bed in the back. The most handsome versions of this toy featured Real Riders wheels, which Mattel installed on the majority of its variations. Production of the Scrambler lasted for six years, with a brief reprise in 1997 as the Trailbuster.

1984

With Real Riders only celebrating their first-year anniversary, Mattel introduced a new wheel: the Ultra Hot. Its sleek, flat, futuristic fantasy design looked like nothing on the road at the time . . . or now, in fact. The Ultra Hot cars were touted as the "fastest breed of Hot Wheels," the exact opposite of the realistic-looking but slow-moving Real Riders. The series launched with a line of 12 vehicles—all renamed old castings except for two: the Sol-Aire CX4 and the Jet

The '65 Mustang Convertible, introduced in 1984, was one of the first Hot Wheels cars to feature the new whitewall tire. The model itself was reasonably well executed and featured an opening hood and detailed engine. But 1950s-style wide whitewall tires were a strange addition. Later versions dropped them in favor of the newer and more realistic five-spoke and seven-spoke wheels.

An immensely popular model, the 1984 Baja Bug remains in the Hot Wheels line today. The first version, pictured here, featured taxi yellow paint and Real Riders wheels.

Sweep X5. For example, the BMW M1 became the Wind Splitter, the Race Bait (Ferrari) 308 became the Street Beast and Quik Trik, and the (Porsche) P-928 became the Predator. Mattel painted each car with Spectraflame-like color-tinted transparent paint, and added the new Ultra Hot wheels. In the years to come, numerous additional castings in the basic line rode on Ultra Hot wheels.

Mattel chose the 1965 Mustang Convertible to be the first new casting introduced with whitewall tires. Identical to the standard blackwalls except for a wide, 1950s-style printed whitewall, these new wheels still featured the chrome-plated mag wheel at the center. The Mustang went on to become one of the most popular Hot Wheels cars ever; 40 variations have been produced to date. These include two California Customs versions and several promotional variations for companies and groups like Fisher Price, the Seattle Toy Show, *Toy Cars and Vehicles* magazine, and the Houston Astros.

Like the Mustang, Mattel used the Sol-Aire CX4 for more than 40 variations since its introduction in 1984. Although not based on a real car, this concept racer has enough real-life styling cues—its sleek body shape, opening rear engine cover, and short, tapered nose—to make it a believable addition to any miniature GT race. Introduced with the futuristic Ultra Hot wheels, later versions, like the blue 1995 Hot Wheels Racing Team, wear the more realistic lace or seven-spoke wheels.

A throwback to the earlier days of Hot Wheels design, this Hot Wheels vehicle was retro before retro became chic. The 1984 Dream Van featured a 1970s-style futuristic cab design and side-opening gullwing door. All versions featured Real Riders wheels.

Mattel introduced another popular model, the Baja Bug, in 1984. First released in yellow with gray Real Riders wheels, the Baja Bug was a perfect choice to wear the oversized tires. This off-road Volkswagen featured a diecast chassis and exposed motor, as well as an engine-cooling air scoop molded into the back of the roof. The Baja Bug has remained almost constantly in the line, with more than 25 variations made to date. Most memorable are the early Real Riders versions in yellow, red, white, or black; a California Custom model painted fluorescent pink; and a Hot Wheels Racing Team variation in the traditional metallic blue.

Mattel also added the Blown Camaro Z-28 in 1984. The company customized this contemporary Camaro with an exposed, "chromed-plastic" engine, metal side pipes cast as part of the chassis, and large wheels in the back. It was introduced in black with handsome gold Hot Ones wheels. Later versions included cars fitted with Ultra Hot wheels and two California Customs: one in red, the other white. Mattel gave the Blown Camaro a new life when, in 1992, the company altered the casting and closed the hood. The revised model was used in the new Pro Circuit line of authentically painted racing cars. The Camaro's appearance benefited tremendously from Mattel's new two-piece racing wheels and realistic paint schemes. The Camaro was again reborn in 1996 as the '80s Camaro, using the same casting from the Pro Circuit cars. Surviving through numerous variations, the '80s Camaro remains in the line today.

Two curious vehicles from 1984 were the Dodge Rampage, a Chevrolet El Camino-like Dodge Omni, and the Dream Van, a futuristic pleasure van designed in what seemed more like the Hot Wheels style of the early 1970s. The Dream Van was a heavy

The 1985 Pontiac Fiero 2M4 featured handsome Hot Ones wheels, first introduced in the early 1980s. Although most Hot Ones wheels are gold in color, Mattel produced some chrome examples during the 1990s.

model—both body and chassis were diecast—and in its several color variations it always rode on Real Riders wheels. Its left side featured a hinged metal door that opened gullwing style. Because of its original design, quality construction, and attention to detail, the Dream Van holds a place among the most memorable of Hot Wheels cars.

Dodge made the Rampage, a pickup truck version of its subcompact Horizon hatchback, from 1982 to 1984. Produced in relatively small numbers, real Rampages have all but disappeared from American roads—all the better that Mattel immortalized it in an accurately rendered miniature.

1985

For 1985, Mattel drastically scaled back its release of new castings. Since 1982, collectors sometimes enjoyed more than 20 new releases per year. In 1985 they only saw six: the Fiero 2M4, Gulch Stepper, Jet Sweep X5, Nissan 300ZX, Tall Ryder, and XT-3. A few more "new" models appeared, but they were only renamed versions of older castings. The Fat Fendered '40 had been the '40s Ford 2-Door, the Good Ol' Pick-Um-Up truck was the '56 Hi-Tail Hauler, and the Mustang S.V.O. began life as the Turbo Mustang. Mattel also introduced the Action Command series of Army machines, but based all six of those vehicles on existing castings of trucks, tanks, and a Jeep.

Of the six new castings, Mattel made two of them—the (Pontiac) Fiero 2M4 and the Nissan 300ZX—very realistic models of the actual cars. The company introduced the Fiero in white with gold Hot Ones wheels and cut a full sunroof into the roof. The Nissan 300ZX featured opening doors, a very unusual move for Mattel. Although many Hot Wheels models feature opening hoods and a few of the futuristic cars have hinged cockpit canopies, the

Mattel rarely included traditional side-opening doors on its Hot Wheels cars. This 1985 Nissan 300ZX features gold Hot Ones wheels and restrained use of tampo decoration. Other models with opening doors included the (Chevrolet) Blazer 4x4 in 1984 and a new 300ZX in 1990.

Mattel introduced a new series in 1986 called Speed Demons. In fact, the six new Speed Demons models were the only new castings that year. Each featured a different animal body mated to a hot rod chassis. The three models pictured here are the Eevil Weevil, Double Demon, and Turboa.

only other original Hot Wheels castings to feature traditional side-opening doors were the Nissan Custom "Z" of 1990 and the Blazer 4x4 of 1984.

1986

Like 1985, Mattel added only six new castings for 1986—all in a new series called Speed Demons. These vehicles featured bodies of animals cleverly melded with mechanical elements such as engines and automotive chassis. The Eevil Weevil had the body of a scorpion with huge diecast exhaust pipes emerging from the sides like legs; the Double Demon was a two-headed dragon with robot-like jointed legs functioning as fenders; and the Vampyra, shaped like a bat, used its pointy face as the car's nose and its legs and wings as fenders. Mattel molded the bodies for all of the Speed Demons in plastic except for the Sharkruiser and Turboa, a coiled snake. Mattel added five more models to this series in the next two years and a few, like the Rodzilla, Fangster, and Turboa, remained in production into the late 1990s.

1987

Both Hong Kong and Mexican production ended in 1987, leaving Malaysia as the primary producer of Hot Wheels cars by the end of the year. Also that year, Michael Strauss, collector and future author of *Tomart's Price Guide to Hot Wheels*, organized the first Hot Wheels convention in Toledo, Ohio. He continues to organize these annual meetings today, and Strauss claims it is the only national Hot Wheels convention in the United States.

Strauss was already publishing a Hot Wheels newsletter, and this was the first year he started including value guides with it. Ultimately, these price guides changed the very nature of Hot Wheels collecting. He published two prices for each car, one for a loose vehicle and the other for one still in its original packaging. The prices listed for blisterpacked cars were often double that for loose cars. From this point on, many

Mattel again experimented with a non-automotive vehicle—this time a 1987 Suzuki QuadRacer. Most early models rode on yellow, first-generation construction tires. This slightly rarer version was fitted with yellow second-generation construction tires that featured spokes instead of holes in the wheel design.

An important model for the Hot Wheels line, the Ferrari Testarossa was originally introduced in solid black with no tampo decoration. Since its introduction in 1987, the Testarossa has seen more than 40 color and wheel variations.

collectors starting keeping their toys unopened, a trend that continues today.

In addition to three new biomorphic Speed Demons, Mattel introduced six new miniatures of real-life vehicles in 1987. Two new Caterpillar trucks were added to the Workhorses series—the Earth Mover and Road Roller—and the Assault Crawler was added to the Action Command series of military vehicles. Mattel introduced the Suzuki QuadRacer, a realistic miniature of a motorcycle-engined all-terrain vehicle. Mattel used the QuadRacer in 1995 to introduce a new wheel known today as the "progressive oval" for its oval-shaped cutouts—each increasing in size—encircling the wheel's center. This wheel has never been used, as of this writing, on another Hot Wheels car.

Perhaps the most important new casting of 1987 was the Ferrari Testarossa. It remains in the line today, having seen more than 40 variations so far. Although Mattel released its Testarossa three

Mattel introduced another important supercar from the 1980s (the real car actually dates from the early 1970s), the Lamborghini Countach. This solid-white car is the first example, made in 1988. Like the Ferrari Testarossa, Mattel decided to omit all tampo decoration to better show off its sleek wedge-shaped Marcello Gandini design.

years after Ferrari introduced the real car, the body style remained current throughout much of the 1990s. The last Testarossa-based Ferrari, the F 512M, was introduced in 1994. Other than exposed headlights, it looked much the same as the original version. Mattel released the first Hot Wheels Testarossa in black with no tampo decoration to mar its sleek lines. This and other early versions rode on the futuristic Ultra Hot wheels; in 1995 the Testarossa, now painted red, was one of the first Hot Wheels models to receive the more realistic five-spoke wheels.

1988

The Hot Wheels brand celebrated its 20th anniversary in 1988 by offering promotional three-packs featuring two cars from the basic line and one with "chrome" or "gold-chrome" plating. Although the vehicles themselves–the Firebird funny car, Ferrari Testarossa, and Letter Getter (van)–were not new, Mattel engraved the words "20th Hot Wheels Anniversary" into the body of each one.

After three rather lean years of new model introductions, Mattel released 12 new castings for 1988. Two of these, the Ratmobile and Rodzilla, were the last additions to the Speed Demons series. Three other models–the futuristic Radar Ranger all-terrain vehicle, the army Rocketank, and the rocket-armed Sting Rod off-road car–all became the latest additions to the Action Command Series launched in 1985.

Another European supercar made its Hot Wheels debut in 1988, the Porsche 959. Although it looked much like a regular Porsche, the real 959 featured four-wheel drive, 450 horsepower, and a top speed of 196 miles per hour.

Following the Hot Wheels Ferrari Testarossa by a year was the Lamborghini Countach, an all-metal version of the 1973 Bertone-designed Italian supercar. Mattel introduced it—the large rear wing and pronounced fender flares mark this Countach as a later version from the mid-1980s—in pure white with no tampo decoration.

Mattel reproduced another supercar in 1988: the Porsche 959. Although the real 959 looked much like a modified 911, its 450 horsepower and four-wheel drive propelled it to 196 miles per hour, making it the fastest car on the road in 1987. Mattel often decorated its 959 in racing stripes and numbers even though the real high-tech GT was never meant for serious racing. A popular Hot Wheels casting, the Porsche 959 is still included in the line today.

Mattel introduced one of its most beautiful "classic" cars in 1988: the French-made 1937 Talbot Lago (pronounced *tal'•bo lah'•go*) Darraq T150C Coupé. The swooping, art deco shape of this intimate two-seat coupe—its flowing fenders and bubble-top roofline tapering to a narrow tail—are reproduced

One of the most beautiful cars ever made, the 1937 Talbot Lago coupe was the epitome of Art Deco style. After a short production run in burgundy, shown here, Mattel switched the color to white, making the early versions more valuable to collectors.

perfectly in 1/64th scale. Originally painted burgundy, Mattel unexpectedly switched the color to white for the rest of its debut year. Today, the burgundy variations command a slight price premium.

By the end of 1988, Mattel had made Hot Wheels cars for 20 years. During this time, production moved from Hong Kong to Malaysia. The basic line of Hot Wheels cars continued to be popular with children and adult collectors, but Mattel was curious to explore the potential of more profitable vehicles. These new models would offer more realism at a higher price.

1989–1994: Upmarket Experiments

1989

Mattel introduced 13 new castings for 1989, a few of which turned out to be very popular with collectors and remained in the Hot Wheels line for more than 10 years.

Mattel also launched a new series called Park 'n' Plates. Advertised as featuring "Collectable License Plate Garages," the Park 'n' Plates series was really a packaging gimmick; no new cars or variations were used. A Park 'n' Plates package included a regular Hot Wheels car and a clear plastic display case with a tinted transparent lid displaying the car's name on raised, painted letters. Mattel discontinued the series in 1991.

Mattel also produced the first Getty Oil Company four-car promotional set. It included the Custom Corvette (1989), Camaro Z-28 (1982), Shadow Jet fantasy racer (1988), and Ferrari Testarossa (1987). Each car featured a prominent Getty logo tampoed onto the body. Mattel and Getty produced a four-car series for three more years. Most models were of contemporary cars—everything from a Nissan 300ZX and Thunderbird Stocker in 1990 to a Mazda Miata and Toyota MR-2 Rally in 1992.

Of the 13 new castings introduced in 1989, more than half have remained in the line (with numerous versions) for over 10 years. Most popular, with 36 variations, was the Custom Corvette. A lightly modified Corvette convertible with ground effects spoilers and side skirts, Mattel introduced the Custom Corvette in dark red metallic with yellow stripes. Some of the more notable variations include the black Getty Oil Company promotional in the same year, a "gold-chrome" Hot Wheels "Billionth Car" commemorative in 1990, and the neon orange or "blue-chrome" California Custom cars of 1990 and 1991. Mattel retired the Custom Corvette in 1999 with a dark blue metalflake Final Run version.

The '32 Ford Delivery truck has seen 30 variations so far. A street rod version of Ford's popular truck, this casting has been used as a promotional vehicle by companies such as Malt-o-Meal, Little Debbie, and Toys 'R' Us, and by groups that include the Early Times Car Club and the Ronald McDonald Children's Charity. Its broad, flat sides and roof lend themselves to large, clear tampoed decorations featuring the company's logo or event information. In

---

The Purple Passion created a sensation when introduced in 1990. It became one of the most popular Hot Wheels cars of all time. Its retro-custom styling appealed to adult collectors who remembered the chopped and channeled customs of their childhood days.

From 1989 to 1992, Mattel produced promotional Hot Wheels vehicles for the Getty Oil Company. Each year, four different cars were specially painted with the Getty logo. One of the first cars was the Custom Corvette. As a new casting for 1989, Mattel painted the Getty version black and the retail version a dark metallic red with yellow and blue tampo decoration.

fact, Mattel used the first version of this 1932 Ford van to promote its Hot Wheels brand by printing the slogan "Hot Wheels Delivery" on each side.

Mattel also introduced its Ferrari F40 in 1989—two years after Ferrari launched the real car. Its miniature diecast V-8 engine is visible through the back window glass, and the hinged metal engine cover opens for a better view. Although a reasonably accurate casting, this model suffered through years of the fantasy-styled Ultra Hot wheels. In 1995 Mattel fitted it with the more realistic-looking five-spoke wheels. Recently, Mattel has been omitting the large tampo decorations on this car. While early versions were painted red and wore yellow "F40" graphics, recent variations have been solid black or yellow with small, tasteful Ferrari logos.

Also produced in 1989 were the VW Bug, School Bus, Ambulance, and Street Roader, a monster-wheeled, high-riding model of the diminutive Suzuki Samurai. Mattel retired the Street Roader in 1999 after 27 variations. The Bug, Bus, and box-style Ambulance continued to thrive during the coming years with varying tampo decoration. In its first 10 years the Ambulance appeared in white, yellow, green, and red, and also functioned as an armored truck, FedEx truck, and postal delivery van. Perhaps the most interesting of the School Bus' 24 variations was the "prisoner transport" police bus, complete with bars painted on the windows. Mattel featured the VW Bug as a limited-edition Treasure Hunt car in 1995; it easily fetches more than $100 today. Recognizing the passion of VW devotees, Mattel has kept the VW Bug almost constantly in the basic line since its 1989 introduction. The company accomplished this partly by including it in six different series: Park 'n' Plates

According to collector Michael Strauss, this '32 Ford Delivery was a miniature of Hot Wheels designer Larry Wood's own truck. A popular casting for promotional use, this first version—from 1989—advertised the Hot Wheels brand.

In 1989, Mattel added the racing-inspired Ferrari F40 to the Hot Wheels lineup. The early version, on the right, featured yellow F40 decoration and Ultra Hot wheels. A recent Mattel/Ferrari licensing deal helped resurrect the F40 in solid red with more realistic five-spoke wheels.

Mattel introduced the California Customs series in 1990. They were more expensive than basic line cars, but featured exuberant fluorescent paint jobs and deluxe wheels, as seen on this BMW 323.

(1991), Pearl Driver (1995), Mod Bod (1996), Biff! Bam! Boom! (1997), Artistic License (1998), and Surf 'n Fun (1999). Of these, perhaps the most interesting was the pearl white version from the Artistic License series, which featured red, green, and black graphics applied in a bold, surrealistic style.

1990

Mattel launched a new series in 1990 called California Customs. A collection of 24 basic line vehicles painted with bright (often fluorescent) colors or "chrome-plated", the California Customs featured wild tampo decorations, deluxe wheels, a sticker sheet, and a button. Because of the ultra-bright body and wheel colors, most of these cars looked more like toys than real customized cars. A few models—the BMW 323 with its blue Turbo Wheels, the 3-Window '34 with its gray Real Riders or "chrome" Turbo Wheels, and the '59 Caddy with its whitewall tires—benefited from the "California Customization" and became miniatures that, with a little imagination, could be seen cruising down Santa Monica Boulevard.

New model production for 1990 dropped to nine, but one new casting surprised even Mattel with its popularity. The Purple Passion, a chopped and channeled early 1950s Mercury coupe, became an instant hit with collectors. Why was this 99-cent car so appealing? Many Hot Wheels cars played on the theme of nostalgia, but this custom had an appealing combination of a gently sloping roof, period Lake (side) pipes, "chrome-plated" custom grille, low stance, and metalflake purple paint. The Purple Passion also featured sleek rear fenders that tapered gracefully into a running-board-like bumper connecting each side of the car, hovering just above the ground. The Purple Passion saw numerous

Like it or not, boom-box cars were—and in some places still are—a symbol of contemporary popular music culture. Always ahead of the curve, Mattel introduced the Mini Truck in 1990. Not only was it a convertible, a style popular at the time, but the entire bed was transformed into one giant speaker platform.

variations, including a Treasure Hunt version in 1995 and a New York Toy Fair model in 1992. But perhaps the most memorable versions are the basic line cars. These include the original one in purple, a green version (the Mean Green Passion), a metalflake-black car from the Steel Stamp Series, and a pearlescent, light purple variation found in the Pearl Driver series. The last three were made in 1995.

Mattel also introduced the Mini Truck in 1990, a wild custom pickup truck. This model captured the essence of 1990s street cruising culture, where music like rap and hip hop prevailed. Cars became the device to spread the chosen tunes across our landscape. Mattel chopped the Mini Truck's top to make it a convertible, a fad popular at the time, then filled the entire bed with stereo and speaker hardware that,

in real life, would be capable of creating a booming bass that could be heard for blocks. Once again, Mattel preserved, in miniature, a little bit of popular history with the Mini Truck.

The first aircraft also entered the Hot Wheels line in 1990. The Propper Chopper, a commercial helicopter, remains in the line today after performing duties for, among others, a couple of make-believe television news stations and three police departments.

1991

According to Mattel, the company manufactured its one-billionth Hot Wheels car in 1991. To mark the occasion it produced a series of four "gold-chrome-plated" Corvettes and placed them on top of a plastic trophy-like stand.

Joining the Countach in 1991 was Lamborghini's new Diablo. Mattel accurately captured its short nose and flattened windshield. Look for the 1997 variation in authentic metallic purple with Lamborghini-like five-hole wheels.

The California Customs were joined by a new series, Super California Customs. These over-the-top customized vehicles featured large, out-of-scale pop-up engines and huge snap-on rear tires. Instead of using regular automotive names, Mattel called these vehicles comical names such as Bod-Acious, Big Sur-Prize, and EZ Duzzit.

A big year for new castings, Mattel introduced 23 models in 1991. Although some—the '59 Caddy, Ferrari 348, Lamborghini Diablo, Mercedes-Benz SL, Porsche 930, Ramp Truck, Toyota MR-2 Rally, and Trailbuster—were destined to see many variations over the decade, none proved to be blockbusters like the Purple Passion.

In fact, some of the models had odd design features that detracted from their appeal. The Cadillac and the Mercedes-Benz SL were too narrow, the elegant BMW 850i wore strange paint colors and featured tan plastic taillights, the Ford Aerostar had "chromed" windows to hide its missing interior, the Limozeen looked cheap with its abundance of "chrome-plated" plastic, the Mazda Miata's shape was too square, and the Trailbuster's body modifications (to distance it from the Jeep Wrangler) made it look awkward.

A few castings were up to the old Hot Wheels standard. The '55 Nomad, a new version of one of the line's early trademark cars, featured a metal chassis and accurately styled single headlights in each fender. Earlier Hot Wheels Nomads had custom vertical quad lights.

Two Ferraris debuted in 1991: the late 1950s 250 Testa Rossa and a contemporary 348. The 250 captured the highly sculpted look of this car's prominent nose, the scooped-out sides of its front fenders, the large fairing behind the driver's head, and its exposed exhaust pipes. The Hot Wheels designers employed a clever trick on the modern 348. They used one piece of plastic to perform two functions in different areas of the car—the rear bumper and contrasting-color seat inserts.

A handsome racing version of Toyota's mid-engined MR-2 featured realistic Toyota graphics and a row of four rally lights along the front bumper.

Featuring trademark Hot Wheels style, Mattel introduced the retro-look Street Beast in 1991. Its fantasy cruiser design was enhanced by styling cues from real cars. Mattel introduced the original Street Beast in turquoise and white. They released the same casting in 1993 as the Swingfire, pictured here.

The Ramp Truck featured a tilting plastic ramp designed to transport a car. Two depressions molded into the ramps kept the car from rolling off. Although the ramp was molded from plastic, the rest of the truck—its large cab and chassis—were diecast metal, making it a hefty model.

Perhaps the most interesting model of 1991 was the Street Beast, a contemporary custom car with a retro-1950s look. Featuring a bullet-nosed front end, rocketship taillights, and two-tone white and turquoise coloring, this classic Hot Wheels fantasy mobile had the inspired design and attention to detail that collectors had come to expect from Hot Wheels cars.

1992

The next year, 1992, presented three new series. Gleam Team cars used existing body styles like the '57 T-Bird, Sheriff Patrol, and Corvette Stingray re-created in plastic with tiny geometric patterns molded over the entire surface. The bodies were then "chrome-plated"—sometimes with a colored tint—and riveted to a diecast metal chassis. The textured surfaces reflected light in different directions, producing an undulating pattern of dark and light areas, not unlike some Op-Art of the 1950s.

Another group of cars used metalflake paint on existing castings like the Zender Fact 4, Limozeen, Lamborghini Diablo, and Talbot Lago. The finish looked like sparkling metalflake fiberglass speedboats of the 1970s, but with multicolored glitter.

The third series was a serious attempt to model some of the popular racing cars of the day. The first Hot Wheels cars to be made in China, Pro Circuit vehicles featured a small assortment of NASCAR, SCCA Trans Am, CART, and NHRA funny cars. The series lasted only two years, with 10 cars issued in 1992—including the Mattel-sponsored Jack Baldwin Camaro—and 7 in 1993. All featured handsome new two-piece wheels and authentic racing graphics. More than twice the price of a regular Hot Wheels car, Pro Circuit racers were still popular with collectors because of their realism.

Mattel introduced the Gleam Team series of cars in 1992. Their plastic bodies had optical patterns molded in, as shown on this '57 T-Bird. When plated with shiny "chrome" (often tinted in different shades) the effect was dazzling.

Mattel started to experiment with limited-edition cars in 1992. While non-limited-edition models were typically made in quantities ranging from 150,000 to 200,000 per color variation, the production figures for the new limited-edition cars were kept below 12,000 units each. These included three versions of the '55 Chevy in stock car form (all from Smokey Yunick's garage) and a white '57 Chevy stock car driven by Fireball Roberts. Mattel also released the Ruby Red Passion, a dark red version of the popular Purple Passion custom Mercury first introduced in 1990. These models only hinted at the numerous future limited editions to pour out of Mattel by the end of the decade.

A few notable new castings appeared in the basic line in 1992. Following the success of the Propper Chopper helicopter of 1990, Mattel introduced a blimp to the Hot Wheels line. It first appeared in gray with the familiar Goodyear logo; a later variation was green and white with Fuji Film markings.

A new casting of the Hiway Hauler delivery truck appeared (the original dated to 1980). Unfortunately, it lost its diecast chassis to a less expensive "chrome-plated" plastic one. Although

"Me, I've built many street and racecars for others and myself. I've stopped doing real cars for a few years now due to other responsibilities, but with my Hot Wheels, I can have as many racecars as I want."
—Michael S. Zarnock, collector, Deerfield, New York

Another new series for 1992 was the Pro Circuit line. Although more expensive than basic line cars, Pro Circuit vehicles featured multicolored authentic racing paint schemes and realistic two-piece wheels. Notice the Hot Wheels-sponsored Jack Baldwin Camaro on the left.

Often called "Dustbuster" minivans, the Chevy Lumina's prominent nose is clearly visible in this photograph. Painted red in 1992, its debut year, later versions were yellow and wore taxi decoration.

never a particularly handsome or realistic casting, the Hiway Hauler—in its original version and with the new model—has probably been used for more product promotions than any other Hot Wheels vehicle. Credit that to its large, flat sides which lend themselves to promotional advertising—everything from Kool-Aid and McDonald's to Wal-Mart and Spam.

The '56 Flashsider, really a 1956 Chevrolet Stepside pickup truck, also appeared in 1992. Its omitted interior could be overlooked because of the accuracy of its body casting. The Flashsider has been through more than 30 variations, including a metallic green Treasure Hunt car in 1997 and a black racing version from the Race Truck series of 1996. The latter is notable for its rarely used black seven-spoke wheels with "Goodyear Eagle" lettering.

A curious model from 1992 is the Chevy Lumina APV minivan. Mattel introduced this typical American minivan in red with a realistically painted (black) section of the forward roof area. This model reappeared as a yellow taxi in 1995.

1993

Perhaps the most important development for Hot Wheels cars in 1993 was the publication of *Tomart's Price Guide to Hot Wheels*. Written by collector Michael Strauss and fully authorized by Mattel, it firmly established the brand as a legitimate collectible and gave fans an insight into the rarity of certain models.

Mattel also celebrated the 25th anniversary of Hot Wheels cars in 1993. The company replicated

Mattel celebrated 25 years of Hot Wheels production in 1993 by reproducing eight cars from the Spectraflame era. One of these was the Classic Nomad, shown here in two shades of metallic blue. The word "Vintage" is molded into the baseplate to avoid any confusion with the original Nomads from 1970. The redline tires are also different; the new ones have an exposed axle at the center.

eight Spectraflame-era models—the Beatnik Bandit, Classic Nomad, The Demon, Paddy Wagon, Red Baron, Silhouette, Splittin' Image, and TwinMill. Like the Pro Circuit cars, Mattel produced the anniversary cars in China. They were originally for sale exclusively in the Toys 'R' Us chain, although some models appeared a few years later in F.W. Woolworth dime stores. Most cars were available in 12 different Spectraflame-like colors and all featured redline tires. They were attached to blisterpacks replicating the original wide, curve-topped cards of the late 1960s, and even included a collector's button, this time in plastic. Fortunately, the cars retained the same quality diecast construction as the originals. It's easy to tell if a car is one of these reissues. All of the new ones have "25th Anniversary" molded into the baseplate.

Mattel introduced three more series in 1993: Revealers, Tattoo Machines, and Demolition Man cars. Revealers, so named because Mattel wrapped the cars in rice paper bags before sealing them in the blisterpack, used the element of surprise to entice buyers. There were 12 models, each available in three color combinations, but there was no way to see what kind of car the package contained unless the paper bag was removed. The only clue was a number on the outside of the bag (1 through 12) so collectors could see that they were buying a different car, even if they didn't know which car. Mattel also used a mail-away prize incentive with the Revealers series. One car in 72 (a case) contained a blue token that could be mailed in and redeemed for a special set of 10 Revealers. About 1,000 packages contained a gold token good for a bicycle and a "gold-chrome-plated" Lamborghini Countach Hot Wheels car.

The Chinese-made Tattoo Machines included 12 models with wild tampo graphics and a sheet of matching temporary body tattoos. Mattel used existing castings but gave them clever new names. For

The 1993 Dodge Viper RT/10 proved to be a bit disappointing with its stubby body casting and limited details. On the left is the original version with Ultra Hot wheels; on the right is a 1999 variation in metallic blue with white stripes and five-spoke wheels. The more realistic wheels and tampo-printed details successfully distract the eye from the inherent deficiencies of this model.

example, the designers decorated the Porsche 959 with eyeballs and renamed it Eye-Gor. The BMW 323 wore tampo-printed skull images and became the Skull Rider. The Talbot Lago had spiders printed all over its white body and its new name became Spiderider.

Mattel based the third series on vehicles found in *Demolition Man*, a science fiction movie that starred Sylvester Stallone and Wesley Snipes. All new castings, they included a vintage Olds 442, a Corvette Sting Ray III concept car, an Oldsmobile Aurora, a Pontiac Salsa concept car, a Pontiac Banshee concept car, a Buick Wildcat concept car, a racing-bodied contemporary Chevrolet Camaro, and two experimental General Motors vehicles. In the film, the characters played by Stallone and Snipes were cryogenically frozen for more than 30 years. As an added feature for these cars, Mattel included with each a "collectable stack & store cryo-cube"—really a clear plastic display case.

The basic line for 1993 included the new Camaro casting used in the Demolition Man series. Called the '93 Camaro, it was actually a racing version with complete roll cage and large spoilers front and rear. Ironically, this car was first released in solid red or purple with no racing graphics. Its racing body had few molded-in details, and it benefited greatly the following year when Mattel painted the car metalflake blue and added Hot Wheels racing graphics.

Mattel also introduced the Dodge Viper RT/10 in 1993. Although anxiously awaited, this model's awkward proportions were a disappointment. It looked

Hot Wheels cars' first designer, Harry Bradley, created the full-size version of the Wienermobile for the Oscar Mayer company. How appropriate that in 1993, 25 years after he left Mattel, one of his designs would again appear in the Hot Wheels lineup. The example pictured here is from 1997, when it was fitted with five-spoke wheels. Early versions featured blackwalls with black hubs.

better in later years when color and wheel changes distracted the eye from its stubby, heavy-looking body. The mold was also revised. Look for the red version with yellow stripes and wheels (1998) or the metallic blue model (1999) featuring white stripes and "chrome" five-spoke wheels.

Two new supercars entered the Hot Wheels line in 1993: the Jaguar XJ220 and the Vector "Avtech" WX-3. Both models featured sleek, accurate castings of these rare and expensive automobiles. Perhaps the most handsome version was the Treasure Hunt XJ220 Jaguar from 1996, which Mattel painted metalflake green and fitted with "gold-chrome" Pro Circuit wheels.

One of the most fun—and popular—Hot Wheels models was introduced in 1993. The Oscar Mayer

"I think the hot dog car [Oscar Mayer Wienermobile] is cool." Why? "Because it's a hot dog!"
—*Jake Serratore, age 5, Los Angeles, California*

Wienermobile was based on a real vehicle that toured the country promoting Oscar Mayer products. Shaped like a hot dog sitting on a bun, this model was an instant hit with Hot Wheels collectors and with fans of popular culture memorabilia.

1994

The Hot Wheels 25th Anniversary series continued for 1994, now renamed the Vintage Collection. Eight more reissues of Spectraflame-era models appeared: the '32 Ford Vicky, Custom Mustang, Deora, Mongoose and Snake funny cars, Mutt Mobile, S'Cool Bus, and Whip Creamer. They now had the word "Vintage" molded into their baseplates instead of "25th Anniversary." Most cars were again available in a number of colors and their packaging still copied the early Hot Wheels blisterpacks.

In 1994, Mattel decided to put its trademarked flame logo somewhere on every car. Usually accomplished with tampo printing, but sometimes molded into window glass or the actual metal, a tiny Hot Wheels logo started appearing on all new models from that year forward.

Other than the eight Vintage Series cars, Mattel introduced five new castings to the basic line for 1994. Of these, the most memorable was the Rigor Motor, a coffin-bodied dragster which became an instant classic. The most handsome versions were the original ruby-red metallic one and a metalflake black variation introduced a year later in the Dark Rider Series: the exposed metal exhaust pipes were painted black, and all of its "chrome" parts—the engine, driver's seat, and bat ornament riding between the front wheels—were plated in black "chrome". It even featured "black-chrome-plated" Pro Circuit wheels.

The No Fear racecar also appeared in 1994. An accurate casting of a mid-1990s Indianapolis-style racer, this car wore the sponsorship logos of No Fear, a sports clothing company. This model reappeared the following year as the Hot Wheels 500 and retired in 2001.

Mattel experimented with new markets during the first half of the 1990s. With California Customs, Pro Circuit racecars, and *Demolition Man* movie vehicles, the company learned that customers were willing to pay more for models that featured more realistic wheels or paint schemes. Mattel also confirmed that the original models from the late 1960s

In 1994, Mattel started adding the Hot Wheels flame logo to every car. Usually tampo printed, the logo appeared in various colors and in different places on different cars. This Vintage-series Nomad wears the Hot Wheels flame on its left rear fender.

The 1994 Rigor Motor became an instant hit upon its introduction. This ruby-red, coffin-shaped dragster featured a metal body, chassis, and sidepipes, as well as a chromed plastic engine and bat ornament mounted between the front wheels. The Rigor Motor remains in the line today.

and early 1970s held a strong nostalgic appeal for adult collectors. The experiments with high-priced limited-edition models, which started in 1992 using a few vintage stock cars and the Ruby Red Passion, showed that the idea of limited edition cars was appealing to collectors, and that people were willing to pay a premium for these vehicles.

Perhaps the most telling event of these five years happened at the start of the decade with the extreme and unexpected popularity of the Purple Passion. This was a car based on 1960s-style customizing, and it clearly appealed to adult collectors who retained fond memories of the cars from that era. Mattel now knew that it had two markets for Hot Wheels cars: children and adults. According to Jim Wagner, senior vice president of marketing for the Hot Wheels brand, 70 to 80 percent of the basic line is still sold to kids. While the company continued promoting the basic line of Hot Wheels cars to children, the second half of the 1990s saw them develop new strategies to stimulate sales of this same line to adults. It also saw the birth of a new collectibles division devoted exclusively to the production of expensive, limited edition vehicles.

1995–Present: Reaching the Adult Collector

1995

Mattel began 1995 with an entirely new system of marketing its basic line of toy cars. The Hot Wheels team succeeded in generating tremendous collector interest in both children and adults. The plan worked so well that the basic structure set in place in 1995 is still used today. It involved three parts: First Editions cars, Treasure Hunt vehicles, and Segment Series cars.

First Editions

For the first time, Mattel created a name for its group of new castings for the coming year. It called them First Editions. All were labeled as such on the front of their blistercards, and Mattel listed the names of more cars in the series on the back of the package. The original Spectraflame Hot Wheels blistercards listed upcoming models, but Mattel had moved away from that device for almost 25 years.

With Mattel once again listing upcoming models on the packaging, collectors could now anticipate all of the new models for the coming year. What would the Dodge Ram 1500 pickup look like? What color would Mattel make the Camaro Convertible? It also made it easy for the collectors to know which new cars they had and which ones they still needed to find. From 1995 to 1997, Mattel introduced 12 new models per year. The idea was to launch a new vehicle each month, but in reality collectors found groups of three or four new cars in releases that occurred every few months.

Some of the more memorable and realistic-looking First Editions included the Camaro Convertible, a metallic turquoise miniature of the contemporary sports car, and a beautifully rendered dark green metallic Dodge Ram 1500 pickup truck featuring a matching green camper top and "chrome" grille. Mattel also introduced a model, in yellow, of the year-old Ferrari 355, a welcome addition to the aging Testarossa. Perhaps the most interesting 1995 First Edition model was not a car, but a boat: the

---

The Hot Wheels team developed an entirely new marketing scheme for 1995 and it remains in place today. They introduced three major groups of vehicles: 1995 First Editions, Treasure Hunt cars, and Segment Series cars. According to Jim Wagner, senior vice-president for Hot Wheels marketing, "This mix is the magic of the Hot Wheels brand." This Dodge Ram 1500 was number 7 of 12 new models introduced that year. It demonstrated a new attention to realism as well, featuring a well-proportioned body, realistic paint color, no gratuitous tampo decoration, "chrome trim", and handsome new five-spoke wheels.

Hydroplane. First introduced in metallic sapphire blue with Hot Wheels Racing Team graphics, this model of a high-speed racing boat inspired non-boat lovers to buy it simply because of its appeal as an accurate miniature.

Treasure Hunt Cars

Twelve Treasure Hunt cars, one released each month, were part two of the new plan. Each featured special paint schemes and deluxe wheel treatments. For example, Mattel painted the Purple Passion in gold metalflake, "gold-chromed" the base and grille, and added gold Real Riders wheels with whitewall tires. The '67 Camaro appeared in white with orange stripes and Real Rider wheels, and the '35 Classic Caddy was metalflake green with black fenders and rode on "gold-chrome-plated" Pro Circuit Indy wheels. Limited to only 10,000 copies each (versus over 100,000 for a regular car), Mattel placed these scarce Hot Wheels cars randomly in the cases that they shipped. In addition to searching for the new cars, Treasure Hunt vehicles prompted collectors to go shopping for cars more often.

During the first few months of distribution, Treasure Hunt cars were found by collectors as planned. But as soon as word got out about the incredible demand for these models, a secondary market developed. Non-collectors started buying them to resell at swap meets and through classified ads in collector publications. Later in the decade, these rare models were most often sold on Internet auction sites such as eBay. Prices quickly jumped from $1 at retail to anywhere from $40 to $200 from

---

"Hot Wheels look fast even when they are in the package."
—Matthew and Gayle Jones, collectors from Hannibal, Missouri

---

these new dealers. Mattel responded by more than doubling the quantity of each Treasure Hunt car in 1996; the count rose from 10,000 to 25,000 for each model. But that was still not enough to control the price gouging that left collectors frustrated and angry. By now, many store clerks knew the value of Treasure Hunt cars. They bought them with their store discount and sold them to desperate collectors for many times the retail price.

Treasure Hunt cars created a tremendous buzz among collectors. Other manufacturers used the same idea—Racing Champions offered "chrome-plated" Chase cars, Johnny Lighting sold white-painted (or white-wheeled) White Lightnings, and in 2000, Mattel-owned Matchbox printed the "Matchbox 2000" logo on the first 10,000 copies of each new model. A new set of Hot Wheels Treasure Hunt vehicles is still released each year, and most continue to end up with high price tags in the secondary market.

Segment Series Cars

The third part of the new marketing plan in 1995 involved making small groups of similarly themed vehicles. Mattel created 12 such groups, and each featured four cars. Of course, the Hot Wheels line had offered vehicle groups before—Super Chromes, Real Riders, Trailbusters, Workhorses, and Gleam Team vehicles, to name a few—but never before had Mattel offered so many new series in one year. It was a clever, cost-saving way to wring more life out of older castings, while generating traffic in the stores. Mattel announced all the new series at the beginning of the year so that collectors could anticipate their arrival in the coming months. If a collector bought a car in one of these series, all of the other cars in the series were listed on the back of the package. Again, Mattel provided the collector with a checklist of what to look for next. Many of the vehicles found in the 12

"I used to live in California, and once at a Target store when the doors opened in the morning I saw collectors get into a fistfight."
—Alex Stephens, age 12, Austin, Texas

groups offered attractive variations of some of the most popular Hot Wheels vehicles.

The 1995 segments were as follows: Race Team Series cars featured Hot Wheels blue paint and the Hot Wheels flame logo; Pearl Driver Series vehicles featured pearlescent paint; Dark Rider Series cars were painted metalflake black and had black "chrome" trim; Krackle Cars Series models had krackle (alligator) finish paint; Steel Stamp Series cars wore dark-colored paint and metallic tampo graphics; Roarin' Rods Series cars featured animal-related tampo decoration; Hot Hubs Series cars rode on special, colored wheels; Speed Gleamers Series cars had "chrome" or "color-tinted-chrome" parts; Silver Series cars were "chrome-plated"; Photo Finish Series vehicles had photographic images printed on their bodies; Racing Metals Series were race-related vehicles with "tinted-chrome" bodies and Hot Wheels racing graphics; and, finally, Real Riders Series cars rode on the deluxe two-piece wheels similar to the ones Mattel first introduced in the early 1980s.

Mattel introduced 12 four-car themed series for 1995. This 1993 Camaro, with its blue-tinted "chrome" finish, was part of the Racing Metals Series.

Mattel revived Real Riders wheels on one of its four-car themed series for 1995. The new Real Riders, however, lost the white "Goodyear" name that had previously been printed on the sidewalls of each tire. This Mercedes Unimog, although not a new casting, was extremely popular because of its fancy new wheels.

Of the 12 groups, the Real Riders Series was without question the most popular because of their realism and the fact that earlier Real Riders (1983) experienced a sharp increase in value. Collectors and speculators snapped them off the shelves and today they sell for $25 to $50 each. The Pearl Driver Series was particularly handsome with its tampo-free, pearlescent-painted cars; the elegant Talbot Lago came in blue, the low-riding Purple Passion in a light purple, the classic VW Bug in pink, and the svelte Jaguar XJ200 in white. The Dark Rider Series was also tampo-free, showing off the four fantasy cars' black-on-black color scheme. The Race Team Series, with its Hot Wheels blue paint and flame logo graphics also proved popular. In fact, Mattel repeated it for three more years—in 1996, 1997, and 1998—each time with different vehicles. Cars included a variety of racing vehicles, from stock cars and funny cars to dragsters and trucks. Curiously, in the first few months of production, Mattel painted the vehicles light blue metalflake. All subsequent Race Team Series vehicles wear darker, metallic sapphire blue paint. Another oddity was that in the first-year series a vehicle called the Side-Splitter wore a Chevrolet bow-tie logo on its hood while the car was actually the Pontiac Firebird funny car casting originally introduced in 1982.

Mattel's Secret Weapon

Mattel's three-part marketing plan—the First Editions, Treasure Hunt cars, and Segment Series cars—energized the Hot Wheels line for 1995. Collectors knew what was coming, and were inspired to search the stores often for new models. But Mattel introduced another, more subtle device to entice the collector: wheel variations.

For 1995, the Hot Wheels line featured a record six new wheel styles. Mattel made no announcement of their arrival and never (except for Hot Hubs) pointed them out on blisterpacks or in series names. The new wheels simply started appearing randomly on different models. They looked more realistic than the 11-year-old Ultra Hot Wheels, and collectors quickly named the different styles: Three-spoke, Five-spoke, Six-spoke, Seven-spoke, Hot Hubs, and Progressive Oval wheels. Of these, the Three-, Five-, and Seven-spoke versions became the standard wheels for most Hot Wheels vehicles.

All of the new wheels featured a realistic concave design where the center of the wheel was recessed. On most cars, the five-spoke design looked the best; a good simulation of a contemporary alloy wheel. The Hot Hubs Series wheels were originally designed for, and used on, the ill-fated Hot Wheels

Perhaps the most beautiful four-car segment for 1995 was the Pearl Driver Series. Each car was painted a different color of pearlescent paint, and, thankfully, no tampo decoration was applied. Clockwise from the top: a Jaguar XJ220, Talbot Lago, VW Bug, and Purple Passion.

Top Speed line. All were of a two-piece design and featured brightly colored hubs on black or colored tires. The six-spoke and progressive oval wheels were also part of this series and haven't been seen on any other vehicles, as of this writing.

In addition to paint and tampo changes, collectors could now look for wheel variations as well. Often, Mattel fitted the same vehicle with several wheel types, greatly multiplying the possible number of variations for any particular car. Very quietly, Mattel had introduced another incentive to bring customers into stores to buy more vehicles. Many collectors were already buying two of every variation—one package to open and one to keep undisturbed. Now, with the added wheel variations, they might buy up to six copies of the same basic car.

1996

Mattel's new plan was so successful in its first year that the company repeated the concept unchanged for 1996. They introduced 12 new 1996 First Editions, 12 new Treasure Hunt cars, and 12 new four-car series. Mattel also started to move more of its production to China. While the Pro Circuit racing cars of 1992 and the reissued "Vintage" cars of 1993 and 1994 were all made in China, in 1996 Mattel started making some of its basic cars in China. Mattel also started issuing numerous old Corgi Jr. castings, and many of them began to enter the Hot Wheels line. All of these were also made in China.

Since Mattel's acquisition of Corgi Toys Ltd. in 1989, Mattel owned the diecasting molds for all the old Corgi Jr. models. Some of these vehicles were quite handsome, and Mattel decided to reissue them as Hot Wheels vehicles. It changed the paint, highlighted details like taillights and grilles, and fitted them with Hot Wheels wheels.

The wheels on Corgi Jr. cars had long been a weak point. Their flat, "chrome-plated" surface looked marginally better than the old Hot Wheels Ultra Hot wheels. Fitted with Hot Wheels five-spoke wheels, their appearance improved dramatically. The cars almost looked like new castings.

For 1996, 14 Corgi Jr. models appeared as Hot Wheels cars. Ironically, several of the models were duplicates of cars already in the Hot Wheels line—the BMW 850i, Corvette coupe, and Ferrari Testarossa among them. But the Corgi BMW featured opening doors and wasn't saddled with the odd-colored plastic taillights of the Hot Wheels version. The Ferrari Testarossa looked stunning in white with a black-painted grille and taillights. Its low, flat stance better replicated the look of the real car than the earlier Hot Wheels casting. And the Mercedes-Benz 500SL was a great improvement over the earlier Hot Wheels version. This one had the proper width (the Hot Wheels SL of 1991 was strangely narrow) and its painted taillights and black-framed windshield added to the realism.

Mattel also gained a number of models that it had never produced—the Ferrari 308 GTS convertible, Ferrari 348TB, and Porsche Targa among them. The Targa was particularly handsome in its neon yellow paint with black Targa roll bar. Corgi's (Austin) London Taxi was reborn in yellow and wore a "See City of Hot Wheels" slogan on its side.

There were other, less exciting models too—like a European Ford Sierra and a bloated Porsche Carrera—but overall the addition of the

Mattel introduced the four-car Race Team Series in 1995. It proved so popular that they continued it with four new cars in each of the next three years. When this Lumina Stocker debuted, Mattel painted it a light metalflake blue. Later the same year it appeared in a deep metallic sapphire blue color.

Corgi Jr. models to the Hot Wheels line-up was a boon to collectors.

Finally, Mattel created three more wheels for the 1996 line: Lace, Directional (sometimes called saw-blade), and Five-hole. Again, any one model could often be found with different wheels. All three of the new wheels featured the concave front surface like the three-, five-, and seven-spoke wheels of 1995. The Lace wheels performed double duty—as a BBS-style racing wheel and as a wire-spoke wheel for vintage cars. The Directional wheels copied the spiral, unidirectional spokes of some American-made aftermarket wheels whose pattern mimicked martial arts throwing stars, and the Five-hole wheels simulated the alloy wheels found on real Lamborghinis. Mattel retro-fitted the Lamborghini Countach and Diablo with five-hole wheels, and in 1997 introduced the 25th Anniversary Countach casting with them. The Five-hole wheels were not limited to Lamborghini models. They could be found on numerous vehicles—everything from a Mercedes-Benz SLK to a Chevrolet C3500 pickup truck.

1996 First Editions

Of the 12 1996 First Editions, the Customized VW Drag Bus created a sensation. It was the heaviest Hot Wheels vehicle ever made, and its large diecast body was attached to a diecast chassis with a hinge at the front, not the rear as is usual. A favorite with Volkswagen as well as Hot Wheels collectors, the VW bus was snapped up by speculators and today can bring over $50 on Internet auction sites such as eBay.

With the acquisition of Corgi Toys Ltd. in 1989, Mattel owned all of the Corgi Jr. diecasting tools. Many of these models appeared as Hot Wheels cars in 1996, 1997, and 1998. One of these was the Corvette coupe, introduced into the Hot Wheels line in 1996. Pictured on the left is an original Corgi Jr. model, made in Great Britain. Notice how its roof was not painted black as it was on the green Hot Wheels version.

A handsome new metallic red-orange Mustang GT convertible debuted, as well as a red Ferrari F50 convertible. With the winged 1970 Dodge Charger Daytona, Mattel produced a famous musclecar that the company neglected in the early days of Hot Wheels cars.

Occasionally, Mattel experimented with plastic-bodied vehicles, and in 1996 the company tried it with the Chevy 1500 pickup truck. Although the model featured a diecast chassis, its accurately molded body was left unpainted except for tampo decoration. Unfortunately, the truck still looked plastic and never became a favorite with collectors.

The 1996 First Editions included a number of trademark Hot Wheels fantasy vehicles, among them the Twang Thang, a concept racer with two miniature guitars integrated into the body; the Dogfighter, a wingless, open-cockpit fighter plane on wheels; the Turbo Flame, a racing vehicle featuring a three-dimensionalized version of the Hot Wheels flame logo; and the Street Cleaver, a hot rod road grader. Perhaps most popular, and in the spirit of classic Hot Wheels humor, was the Radio Flyer Wagon. Licensed by the popular brand of childhood wagon, this model was souped up and hopped up with an oversized "chromed" plastic engine in the back and exposed side exhaust pipes cast as part of its diecast chassis.

Treasure Hunt Cars

The Treasure Hunt cars continued to be more detailed versions of basic cars. For example, Mattel painted the Dodge Ram 1500 pickup a rich dark red metallic, added "chromed" Real Riders wheels, and painted black the recessed areas on the "chrome" grille. It made a white version of the Dodge Viper RT/10 and painted blue stripes down the body's center. It also rode on white, two-piece Indy-style wheels first seen on the Pro Circuit cars. Mattel used "chromed" versions of the Pro Circuit Indy wheels on a metallic blue '37 Bugatti. It was interesting for collectors to see how the same wheels, painted different colors, could look as natural on a contemporary sports car as they did on a classic like the Bugatti.

Segment Series Cars

Once again, Mattel announced 12 new four-car series for 1996. Three popular ones continued from 1995: the Race Team Series, Dark Rider Series, and Silver Series. The nine others included Race Truck Series, featuring racing graphics applied to pickup trucks and a semi truck; Flamethrowers Series, all with flame graphics; Space Series, featuring futuristic vehicles; Mod Bod Series, wearing brightly colored tampo decorations of flowers and messages of peace and love; Sports Car Series, which had sports-themed graphics; Splatter Paint Series, featuring speckled paint finishes; Street Eaters Series, with graphics of open mouths with sharp teeth; Fast Food Series, which used images of food like pasta and pizza over each car's entire body surface; and the Fire Squad Series, a series of fire rescue vehicles.

A few of the more interesting models included, from the Mod Bod series, a bright pink Hummer painted with flowers and the words "peace" and "love," and the entire Race Truck Series. Three of these models, a Dodge Ram 1500 pickup, Kenworth T600, and '56 Flashsider (Chevy pickup) featured unusual black Seven-spoke wheels (normally the wheel center was "chromed") with yellow "Goodyear" and "Eagle" markings on the sidewall.

1997

Mattel continued the three-part marketing strategy (First Editions, Treasure Hunt cars, and 1997 Segment Series Cars) for 1997. And the company also started new programs that added different types of cars to the brand. One of these new programs was real-life racing.

In the spirit of designer Larry Wood's Special Delivery (mailbox) car from 1971, the 1996 Radio Flyer Wagon turned a nonmotorized object into a humorous fantasy racer, complete with side pipes, "chrome-plated" engine, and giant wing. Cars in a similar vein would follow in the coming years. These included the Express Lane (grocery cart), the Hot Seat (toilet) in 1998, and the Baby Boomer (carriage) in 1999.

In 1997, Mattel reentered the racing world in a big way. Sponsoring Kyle Petty's NASCAR Pontiac Grand Prix paved the way for Mattel's new Pro Racing series of stock cars. For several years, two companies—Racing Champions and Racing Collectibles—had cornered the market on 1/64th-scale licensed NASCAR diecast vehicles. Mattel decided to join the NASCAR frenzy and produce its own cars.

The company divided the Pro Racing line into two parts: one for adults and one for children. The kids' cars were less expensive (about $2), and featured plastic base plates and one-piece plastic tires. For about a dollar more the collector cars featured a metal chassis, separate, soft plastic tires, and came packaged with a trading card. The front of the card featured a photo of the driver with his car; driver statistics were on the back. Body castings were based on NASCAR-approved styles for that year—a Monte Carlo, Thunderbird, and Grand Prix. All paint schemes were authentic.

The Pro Racing line was a completely different concept for the Hot Wheels brand. For the first time, the goal was to reproduce the cars as true to the original as possible. The Hot Wheels basic line had always been about altering and customizing vehicles in some way, but NASCAR fans demanded realism and Mattel gave them what they wanted.

Mattel also introduced a new line of highly detailed 1/64th-scale models called Hot Wheels Collectibles. Car customizer Boyd Coddington's series of four cars—the Vern Luce Coupe, CheZoom, Smoothster, and CadZZilla©—had been introduced a year earlier and were sold through the mail only. But they were just an exercise to prepare for a new line of collectible cars to be launched in 1997. These new cars featured more parts than basic line cars, two-piece wheels, and details like head and taillights painted silver or red. The first Hot Wheels Collectible cars—a '50s Buick Woody, '38 Ford Cabover truck, 1965 Shelby Daytona, and a Dodge Viper GTS—were sold in sets of two vehicles. By the next year, collectors found many models packaged individually. The quality construction of Hot Wheels Collectible cars does not come cheaply; prices range from $8 to $10 each.

Mattel acquired the Tyco company in 1997, owner of the Matchbox brand. Speculation started immediately about the fate of Matchbox. If it survived, how would Mattel distinguish it from the Hot Wheels brand? Frankly, Matchbox needed an infusion of new ideas. In the mid-1990s its line had grown stale compared to Hot Wheels cars. There was little collector buzz because there weren't many new models or even variations of old ones. Time has shown that the Mattel purchase of Tyco was beneficial

Part of the four-car Mod Bod Series for 1996, this plastic-bodied hot pink Hummer ironically featured tampo decorations of peace signs, doves, and the words peace and love.

to the venerable Matchbox brand. The number of new model introductions for 1999 and 2000 rose dramatically, and themed series, like the Hot Wheels four-car series, gave new life to existing castings. The two brands seem to exist well together. Mattel makes clear distinctions between the two, making Matchbox the more realistic line designed for "Real Driving Adventure!" and Hot Wheels vehicles the sexy line featuring "speed, power, performance, and attitude."

1997 First Editions

Mattel acknowledged the popular lowrider culture with the '59 Chevy Impala. It featured fender skirts and deep metallic pink paint with a complex orange pinstripe design tampoed on each side. Another vintage vehicle—this time a motorcycle—appeared in 1997. The Scorchin' Scooter could have been a custom job from the 1950s or a tricked-out design from the late 1990s. Its low-and-cool looks and mostly metal construction made it a favorite among collectors.

Mattel also introduced the 1970 Plymouth Barracuda. Other than the Snake funny car, the last Barracuda offered by the Hot Wheels line was the original Custom Barracuda in 1968. The new model was a Hemi-engined convertible, painted lime green. Another instant hit with collectors, this model was extremely hard to find during its first few months of production.

Mattel updated two of its most popular models, the Corvette and the Lamborghini Countach. Originally introduced in metalflake aqua with Lace wheels, the Corvette accurately replicated the new body style of America's favorite sports car. This Hot Wheels vehicle was one of a few to have the Hot Wheels flame logo molded into the rear window glass rather than painted on. The 25th Anniversary Lamborghini Countach, so named to celebrate Lamborghini's 25th birthday in 1988, represented the last version of the Countach to be sold before being replaced by the Diablo. This Hot Wheels casting had crisper details than the original Hot Wheels Countach from 1988, making it a fine miniature example of a classic Italian supercar.

Although not part of the 12 1997 First Editions series, more than 10 new Corgi Jr. castings entered the Hot Wheels lineup for 1997. Some, like the Road Roller and the racing Jaguar XJR40, were made for the European market only. While most of the models destined for the United States were not as interesting as the Corgi Jr. cars introduced the previous year, a few, like the Land Rover Mark II (utility truck) and Mercedes-Benz 190E and 300TD (wagon) are nicely crafted models of everyday European vehicles.

Treasure Hunt Cars

Mattel started using more fantasy vehicles such as the Street Cleaver, Dogfighter, and Rail

In 1997 Mattel reentered the world of racing sponsorship in the biggest way since their funding of the Snake and Mongoose funny cars in the early 1970s. Kyle Petty's Hot Wheels Pontiac Grand Prix gave Mattel a much-needed entrée into NASCAR, one that had been dominated in the mid-1990s by other manufacturers like Racing Champions and Racing Collectibles. The Hot Wheels Pontiac is pictured on the right. Soon, NASCAR-themed vehicles—everything from Thunderbirds and Monte Carlos to motorcycles, buses, and Suburbans—started appearing in the Hot Wheels Racing line.

Rodder for the 1997 Treasure Hunt cars. The few vehicles based on real cars reverted to using standard wheels. The '56 Flashsider (Chevrolet pickup) had Five-spoke wheels and a paint scheme like one that could be found on any basic line car, the Olds Aurora also wore Five-spoke wheels and metallic purple paint, and the Mercedes-Benz SL was solid black with regular Five-spoke wheels. Even though demand was still high because Treasure Hunt cars were hard to find, the models themselves offered no special features and consequently no real added value.

Segment Series Cars

Of the 12 new four-car series for 1997, the only carry-over theme was the Hot Wheels Race Team. The other 11 were Speed Spray Series, featuring mud, salt, and water spray graphics; Heat Fleet Series, using flame graphics; Quicksilver Series, wearing tampo decorations of weather words ("hurricane," "blizzard," and the like) and related graphics; Blue Streak Series, candy-blue painted vehicles; White Ice Series, white-painted, tampo-free cars; Phantom Racers Series, featuring transparent, tinted plastic parts; Dealer's Choice Series,

Mattel officially launched the Hot Wheels Collectibles line in 1997. Cars in this series featured more parts, deluxe wheels, and realistic tampo-printed details. The AMX first appeared in 1999 painted lime green as part of a two-car set. Later in the year, it could be found in this deep periwinkle blue and packaged individually. The price for more realism was steep, however; brand-new in the package Hot Wheels Collectibles cars usually sold for $8 to $10 each.

displaying playing card graphics; Rockin' Rods Series, with rock music graphics; Street Beast Series, with animal graphics; Biff! Bam! Boom! Series, with their bold cartoon-like word graphics; and Spy Print Series, featuring espionage-themed graphics.

Of the 12 series, the Hot Wheels Race Team (now in its third year) was still one of the most handsome. Using a Hummer, Chevy 1500 pickup, 3-Window '34 (Ford), and an '80s Corvette, the sapphire blue metallic paint combined with the Hot Wheels red and yellow logo made for four very appealing vehicles. The White Ice Series provided an interesting contrast to the Dark Riders Series from the two previous years—their solid white paint and tinted "chrome" parts gave them a ghostly appearance. Perhaps the most intriguing new series was the Blue Streak Series. The smooth, deep blue finish on these vehicles had a mirror-like quality and depth rivaled only by some of the original Spectraflame colors.

1998

The Hot Wheels brand reached its 30-year anniversary in 1998. Mattel celebrated by reissuing 30 popular models—one for each year from 1968 to 1997. Vehicles included a mixture of real cars and Hot Wheels fantasy originals. From the early years, Mattel chose the Deora, Ford Vicky, and Nomad; later years were represented by the Dodge Viper RT/10, VW Bus, and Scorchin' Scooter. Original colors were replicated, as well as original packaging designs.

Mattel expanded the Pro Racing line to include models in larger scales: 1/43rd and 1/24th. With the basic line, the company continued to use the structure set in place in 1995: 1998 First Editions, Treasure Hunt cars, and Segment Series cars.

1998 First Editions

Since 1995, Mattel had introduced 12 new cars each year. For 1998 it introduced 40. The variety was enormous, and included everything from classic

> "To maintain an ongoing interest in the Hot Wheels brand, we try to consistently focus on kids, which creates a long-term collector base. We also try to keep the brand relevant to car enthusiasts."
>
> —Jim Wagner, Senior Vice President, Marketing, Hot Wheels

By 1997, the lowrider craze was already well established in Southern California and New Mexico. Mattel launched the '59 Chevy Impala and helped bring this uniquely American cultural phenomenon to the rest of the country. It was joined the following year by the '65 Chevy Impala lowrider, a beautifully rendered coupe with Gold Lace wheels and sparkling metallic purple paint. These cars were not especially fast on Hot Wheels track, as their low-hanging bumpers dragged the surface when negotiating a loop-the-loop.

convertibles, musclecars, and minivans to contemporary sports cars, racing trucks, and trademark Hot Wheels concept cars. Most of the new castings exhibited a new level of realism and detail.

Mattel included 16 racing vehicles. Most notable was the Go Kart, a diminutive high-speed racing kart, and the first go kart Mattel ever made. Other racers included several contemporary vehicles—a Callaway C7, a Ford Escort Rally, an IROC Firebird, a Pikes Peak Celica, a Mustang Cobra, the Slideout sprint car, and a Panoz GTR-1. All of these were accurately cast, realistic models and will someday be a vivid record of the variety of racing styles prevalent in the late 1990s.

Mattel included a few vintage racers, too—the Chaparral 2 from 1963 and the famous Jaguar D-Type, which won the 24 Hours of Le Mans in 1955, 1956, and 1957. The Lakester, a 1960s-style salt-flat racer, was unique because its clamshell body, hinged on the side, opened to reveal two miniature engines.

Three vintage cars entered the line—the '63 T-Bird, complete with Speedster tonneau (covering the back seats), the '70 Roadrunner, and the 1970 Mustang Mach I. The Thunderbird was an excellent model of a long overlooked classic. (Husky made the only other one in the mid-1960s.) The Hot Wheels model featured fender skirts and a heavy metal chassis with diecast grille, bumpers, and taillights. The Hemi-engined orange and black Plymouth Roadrunner and the yellow Mustang Mach I both featured plastic base plates. This reduced their weight, and they actually ran faster on Hot Wheels track than some Hot Wheels cars with metal chassis.

There were five customized vehicles for 1998: the '65 Impala lowrider, Customized Chevrolet C3500 pickup truck, Dairy Delivery, Tail Dragger, and '32 Ford. Based on a vintage delivery truck, the Dairy Delivery created a sensation with its pearl white paint and raked stance. The '65 Impala lowrider, first introduced in metalflake purple with yellow graphics, was right-on as far as body proportions, details, and its low-riding stance. In fact, the car was so low that its bumpers dragged the track and slowed it considerably when attempting a Hot Wheels loop-the-loop. The Tail Dragger, in the spirit of the Purple Passion, was based on a 1941 Mercury coupe. Its body was chopped and lowered, giving it a typical "lead sled" look, and realistically painted in dark purple metalflake. Mattel thankfully kept the tampo printing to a minimum, adding only a few appropriately scaled pinstripes.

An immediate hit with collectors, the '70 Plymouth Barracuda convertible was difficult to find in stores during its first few months of production. Nostalgic adults picked them up as fast as they could find them. Later versions appeared in black, purple, and orange, but the handsomest was the original lime green model with Five-spoke wheels, pictured here.

The Hot Wheels line, always known for its fantasy concept cars, added eight in 1998. Reminiscent of the early Hot Wheels style, the Double Vision was a twin-bodied, catamaran-like car with two engines mounted on one side and the driver's seat on the other. Fathom This was a small, futuristic *submarine*, something new for the Hot Wheels line. Whatta Drag, using a body based on the 1950s BMW Isetta microcar, grafted a hugely out-of-proportion blown racing engine on the back, and replaced the stock Isetta's two tiny rear wheels with one massive slick. Two other models, following the tradition of the Radio Flyer Wagon of 1996, used everyday objects as the basis for humorous fantasy hot rods. The Hot Seat featured a miniature toilet, complete with an engine sitting in the tank and a plunger for a steering wheel. The Express Lane cleverly integrated a red plastic grocery cart with a diecast metal chassis and engine to make the world's first miniature hot rod grocery cart.

And finally, Mattel made arrangements with Chrysler, Ford, and California State University to reproduce some of their contemporary concept cars. The Cal State Solar Eagle III won the General Motors-sponsored intercollegiate solar car race "Sunrayce" in 1997. Mattel accurately reproduced its sleek, flat body and blue foil-like solar panels covering most of its broad top surface. Mattel also included a Ford GT-90, showcasing Ford's "new edge" design philosophy of the late 1990s, and three Chrysler concept cars: the futuristic Thunderbolt coupe, the Dodge concept sports car, and the Dodge Sidewinder pickup truck.

Treasure Hunt Cars

Mattel chose a number of fantasy castings for the 12 Treasure Hunt cars. Although it included a few reality-based vehicles like the 3-Window '34 and the '57 Chevy, none of the new Treasure Hunt

Mattel introduced the '97 Corvette the same year the real car made its debut. This was the fifth-generation Corvette, and the Hot Wheels model accurately replicated its massive width and broad rear haunches. Look closely at the rear window of this miniature to see the Hot Wheels flame logo molded into the glass. This is one of the few models to feature the logo this way; on others, it's painted.

cars—fantasy or otherwise—featured special wheels or intricate tampo markings. Perhaps the most interesting was the Road Rocket, a futuristic racer with a "chrome" body wearing a clear plastic overlay and "TH-98" tampoed on each side. The combination of a clear plastic and "chrome-plated" body gave it an icy cold look.

Segment Series Cars

The fourth Race Team Series arrived with the same handsome blue paint schemes. In 1998, Mattel chose a Shelby Cobra 427 S/C, '63 Corvette, '67 Camaro, and Mercedes-Benz C-Class, the first true foreign car ever chosen to represent the Hot Wheels Race Team. (The Baja Bug was used as a Race Team vehicle in 1996, but its racing modifications gave it a uniquely American look.)

Other than the Tech Tones Series, a group of concept and fantasy cars painted with dark, blotchy, high gloss paint schemes, the 10 additional series for 1998 relied heavily on tampoed graphics to define each four-car group. The Tattoo Machines Series cars wore stylized patterns of waves and spirals, Techno Bits Series cars had computer-related graphics printed on futuristic fantasy cars, Tropicool Series vehicles featured bright colors with beach-themed graphics, Low 'n' Cool Series cars had a lowrider stance and pinstripe graphics, Biohazard Series vehicles had toxic waste graphics, Dash 4 Cash Series cars were racers with bank and currency images tampoed on them, Mixed Signals Series vehicles had a hodgepodge of signage graphics printed on them, Flyin' Aces Series cars had military airplane graphics and simulated riveted panels painted on, and Sugar Rush Series vehicles wore the logos of famous candies like Butterfinger and Nestle's Crunch. The other group, and arguably the most interesting, was called the

Artistic License Series. Its vehicles featured tampoed artwork in the style of famous artists.

1999

In 1999, Mattel signed a deal with Ferrari for the exclusive rights to reproduce Ferrari miniatures in all scales. Collectors worried about how the deal might affect their model collecting. Would they have as large a choice? Would they be able to find the quality they were used to from model makers like Bburago and Maisto, which specialized in 1/18th-scale cars? For Hot Wheels-sized toys the prospects were less frightening. Mattel already owned both of the major brands of 1/64th-scale diecast: the Hot Wheels line and Matchbox.

By the end of 1999 it was clear that the Ferrari/Mattel deal was good for Hot Wheels collectors. Four new models were introduced—the 360 Modena, 456M, F355 Spider, and F50 Berlinetta—all in red and all carefully and accurately made. Older Ferrari castings, like the F355 Berlinetta and F40, appeared in new colors. And more would follow in 2000.

Other than the Ferrari deal, 1999 saw numerous new castings added to the collectibles line. Initially,

In 1998, the Hot Wheels brand's 30th anniversary, Mattel released 40 new castings instead of the usual 12. Among them was the diminutive Go Kart. This was the first such vehicle ever included in the Hot Wheels line, and it proved to be immensely popular. Mattel painted the first version bright green; the following year it appeared in orange.

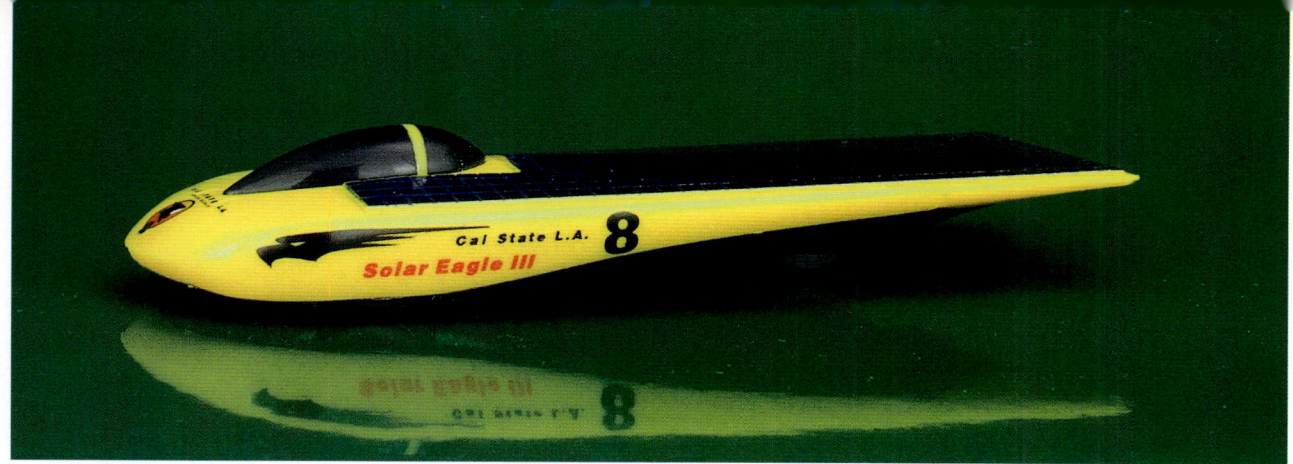

Among the 40 new castings for 1999 was the Solar Eagle III, a solar-powered racing car that won the 1997 intercollegiate Sunrayce. Its delicate, aerodynamic body was expertly reproduced, including blue foil-like solar panels covering most of its top surface.

Mattel made most of the vehicles available in two-, three-, and four-car sets; later in the year some castings started turning up individually. Some of the new sets for 1999 included reproductions of cars from the collections of baseball great Reggie Jackson and television talk show host Jay Leno, Smoke 'n' Water (a pickup truck and a boat), Hard Rock Café (three vintage Cadillacs), and two pairs of musclecars.

1999 First Editions

Mattel released 26 new models in 1999. This number does not include the Ferrari 456M, F355 Spider, and F50 Berlinetta mentioned earlier, as they were added later in the year, after Mattel had already announced the 1999 First Editions series. Official 1999 First Editions cars again included a wide variety of vehicle types—everything from classic cars and racers to real Detroit concept cars and trademark Hot Wheels fantasy vehicles.

Interestingly, Mattel introduced a classic 1936 Cord sedan. The company issued a Cord in 1971, but it was a two-door model and featured a custom engine sticking through the hood. Mattel also debuted the '38 Phantom Corsair. The real car was a prototype designed by Rust Heinz, a member of the H. J. Heinz family. It featured aerodynamic styling, front-wheel drive, and safety padding inside. Shortly after the car was completed, Mr. Heinz died, and the car was never put into production. The other "classic" was a 1970 musclecar, the Chevelle SS. A large, weighty model with both a diecast body and chassis, it was handsome but not a good performer on Hot Wheels track. Mattel released the Chevelle in metallic navy with white stripes. A later and rare version was metallic gold with black stripes. Less rare is the gold version with a "chromed-plastic" chassis.

Racing vehicles played an important part of the 1999 lineup. Vintage racers like the classic Ford

---

"I like the Solar Eagle because I can put a car on the back and it works like a flatbed [truck]."
—*Jake Serratore, age 5, Los Angeles, California*

Mattel introduced the Dairy Delivery in 1998 to rave reviews from collectors. Its body was gently raked and painted in gleaming white pearl lacquer.

GT40 and Shadow Mk IIa Can Am car appeared with new models like the Olds Aurora GTS-1, Porsche 911 GT3 Cup, Mercedes-Benz CLK-LM, and Pikes Peak Tacoma.

One of the year's most popular models, the Phaeton, was a chopped-top 1920s-style convertible, sleekly customized with a raked back grille, removable top, and exposed side exhaust. This model exhibits the best kind of classic Hot Wheels customization. In fact, the Phaeton was chosen as one of the four *Hot Rod* magazine Series cars in 2000. Two other custom cars were also introduced in 1999: the Track T and the '56 Ford truck. The Track T's low-slung styling, perfect weight balance, and compact size made it one of the fastest Hot Wheels cars ever. The '56 Ford truck (in fact a panel delivery truck) teased collectors with a hood that barely opened.

Another favorite model for 1999 was the Tee'd Off, a hot rod version of a typical golf cart. Sporting a giant "chromed-plastic" engine behind the seats, this comical model continued the Hot Wheels humor found in recent vehicles like the Radio Flyer Wagon, Express Lane (grocery cart), and Hot Seat (toilet).

Finally, Mattel continued its relationships with General Motors and Chrysler by offering models of several real concept cars. The Monte Carlo Concept Car was really a miniature of the Intimidator, a styling study previewing the new NASCAR Monte Carlo. The Pontiac Rageous was a sporty, multipurpose car featuring a rear liftgate and a drop-down tailgate. Mattel represented Chrysler designs with a beautifully detailed Jeepster, complete with painted side-window frames and open roof, and with the Pronto Cruiser concept car.

Treasure Hunt Cars

Mattel introduced another 12 cars, but like the year before, the colors and wheels were similar to mainline cars. Perhaps the most handsome model was that of a red Mercedes 540K, even though it wore basic Five-spoke wheels. This was a strange choice, knowing that a 1994 version made for FAO Schwarz looked so good with Pro Circuit Indy wheels and a 1997 variation in the European Classics set featured handsome Real Riders wheels.

Segment Series Cars

For the first time since Mattel introduced the four-car, themed series in 1995, the Hot Wheels Race Team was not included. As in 1998, most of the series relied almost exclusively on tampo graphics to define them. Two notable exceptions were the Surf 'n' Fun Series, which, along with surfing-related graphics, used California beach cars such as the Woody, Nomad, and VW Bug. The other was the Pinstripe Power Series, which featured cars like the 3-Window '34 Ford, Tail Dragger, and '65 Impala wearing a heavy dose of pinstripe tampo.

The 10 other groups were the Buggin' Out Series, featuring cars with insect graphics; X-Ray Cruisers Series, where an outline of each vehicle's interior structure was printed on its surface; Street Art Series, where the vehicles displayed graffiti-like graphics; Game Over Series, a group of cars with video game graphics; X-Treme Speed Series, with designs featuring youth sports like snowboarding and dirt biking; Mega Graphics Series, with large-scale tampo designs; Terrorific Series, featuring horror-related graphics; Classic Games Series, wearing logos of family games like Uno, Skip-Bo, and Toss-Across; Sugar Rush II Series, featuring more candy logos; and Car-Toon Friends Series, featuring television cartoon characters from the Rocky and Bullwinkle show of the 1960s.

2000

For 2000, Mattel again employed the First Editions, Treasure Hunt, and Segment Series plan. It also expanded the line of authentic racing vehicles. In fact, the Hot Wheels website featured racing vehicles more prominently than either the mainline cars or the children's section.

The NASCAR 1/64th-scale line continued for 2000. The basic cars featured plastic wheels and could run on traditional Hot Wheels track. Mattel offered four series of more detailed cars: Deluxe, featuring a metal chassis and soft plastic tires; Trackside, which were sold mostly at hobby stores and actual NASCAR races; Select, featuring cars mounted in a plastic display case; and Crew's Choice, offering opening hoods and lift-off bodies to better see the detailed driver's cages and engines.

Mattel also introduced a Treasure Hunt series within the NASCAR line. These special stock cars wore graphics commemorating famous race tracks such as Daytona, Darlington, and Talledega.

Within the Deluxe segment of NASCAR racers, Mattel produced 10 limited edition four-car sets. These series, which used castings from basic cars and included models such as school buses, go karts, motorhomes, helicopters, Chevrolet Suburbans, and hot rods, all wore authentic NASCAR graphics and were more detailed than the average mainline car. Mattel packed these vehicles randomly within boxes of Deluxe segment cars, and gave collectors another reason to visit the stores often.

Also new for 2000 was a line of 1/64th-scale Grand Prix racers, all made to run on Hot Wheels track. Major teams like Jaguar, Jordan, McLaren, Williams, and of course Ferrari, were represented.

2000 First Editions

Mattel introduced 36 new models for 2000, and again included a wide variety of racing and classic cars,

In 1999, Mattel signed an exclusive licensing deal with Ferrari that allowed the toy company to be the sole producer of Ferrari models. New Ferraris started appearing by the end of the year. This prompted 12-year old collector, Alex Stephens, to innocently tell me, "There are a lot of red cars this year." Among them were the F355 Spider (front row), 456M (far left), F50 Berlinetta (far right), and 360 Modena (back). Mattel added the vintage (1968) 365 GTB/4 "Daytona" in 2000.

Hot Wheels fantasy cars, reality-based customs, and a couple of realistic concept cars and stock vehicles.

Two of the most beautiful Hot Wheels cars ever made, the Phantastique and the Thomassima III, made their debut in 2000. Inspired by the French-made 1938 Delahaye Type 165 roadster, the Phantastique captures the essence of this "fantastic" art deco masterpiece. For its breathtaking body design, this exotic and rare (only two were made) car is often included in lists of the most important automobiles of the twentieth century. Mattel appropriated its flowing fenders, hidden wheels, pinched midsection, tapered tail, and "chrome" wind-split running down its long hood to divide the windscreen. The company painted the Phantastique a brilliant peacock blue metallic and avoided distracting tampo designs.

The Thomassima III was an actual car built by an American, Tom Meade, in the late 1960s. He based its running gear on a Ferrari 250GT, and built a custom body featuring a long, tapering hood, large gill slits behind the front wheels, "spaghetti" sidepipes (a Meade invention), and canopy-style cockpit. Mattel beautifully rendered his design in dark red metalflake, and it is the only known 1/64th-scale model of this important sports car.

Mattel also modeled several other classic cars—the 1967 Dodge Charger R/T and 1964 Lincoln

A real car built by American Tom Meade, the exotic Thomassima III was recreated for the 2000 Hot Wheels line. The actual car's mechanicals were based on a Ferrari 250GT; the custom body was designed by Meade in the late 1960s. Notice his signature "spaghetti pipes" exiting below the front fender.

Mattel introduced its hot rod golf cart, the Tee'd Off, in 1999. This cleverly designed fantasy vehicle deftly kept the spirit of a real-life golf cart while adding an oversized "chrome-plated motor" in the rear. The Tee'd Off is an example of the kind of humor that has kept Hot Wheels cars intriguing and amusing to both children and adults for more than 30 years.

> *"Hot Wheels are something that can take me away from the stress of the adult world where everyone at work and home depends on you to be the pillar of strength and to make all the right decisions. Hot Wheels relax me and bring me back to the easygoing childhood I once knew."*
> —Michael S. Zarnock, collector, Deerfield, New York

Continental among them. Dodge designed the '67 Charger—the first Charger—with an aerodynamic fastback roof to better compete on the NASCAR circuit. The Hot Wheels Charger was the first 1/64th-scale model ever made of this important musclecar.

The Hot Wheels line rarely included a box-stock four-door car, but in 2000 Mattel introduced the elegant, knife-edged, slab-sided 1964 Lincoln Continental Convertible. Jacqueline Kennedy drove a white Continental Convertible, and rode in a dark blue one on that fateful day, November 22, 1963. Interestingly, Mattel painted the prototype for this model black because it was originally designed to be part of a Presidential Action Pack that was subsequently dropped.

Eight more racing cars appeared in 2000, most notably the Metrorail, a dragster version of Nash's diminutive Metropolitan, and the Lotus Elise 340R, a miniature of Lotus' limited-production racer based on the popular Elise sports car. Reality-based customs included a handsome Deuce roadster with a shiny bare metal finish, a stout little Anglia Panel Truck, a 1953 Buick called So Fine, and an Austin Healey roadster.

More than 10 classic Hot Wheels fantasy vehicles debuted, including a new, low-slung motorcycle called Blast Lane; the Deora II, a redo of the original Dodge-based show-truck; the Muscle Tone, a modern interpretation of the 1967 Camaro; the MX48 Turbo, the roadster driven by Mattel's own Max Steel action

One of the most beautiful cars of the 1960s, Mattel's '64 Lincoln Continental showcases the flat-surfaced, knife-edged design that defined an era of automotive production. Jacqueline Kennedy drove a white Continental much like this model, and of course rode in the back of a dark blue one on that fateful day in November 1963.

Treasure Hunt Cars

After several years of bland Treasure Hunt cars, Mattel returned to its original style of offering some models with special wheels. For 2000, the '36 Cord, Double Vision, Ford GT-40, Go Kart, '57 T-Bird, and '67 GTO all featured Real Riders wheels. The GTO itself was special; before 2000 this car was only available in sets and as a promotional vehicle. Mattel also started the new practice of tampo-printing a common logo on most Treasure Hunt cars. It featured a five-pointed star with the characters "TH" and "2000."

Segment Series Cars

For 2000, Mattel again issued 12 four-car themed series. There were no carryovers from 1999, and most of the series relied on graphic decoration to distinguish themselves. A couple of exceptions were the *Hot Rod* magazine Series and the Virtual Collection.

The Hot Rod group paired appropriate hot rod castings like the Phaeton and Tail Dragger with classic flame decoration. This group was an immediate hit with collectors. The other series, called the Virtual Collection, was aimed at children. Printed on the blisterpack behind each car was a string of numbers and/or letters. When entered into a box on a special page of the Hot Wheels website, they granted the user rights to download a screensaver depicting the vehicle they purchased. Originally designed to include four cars in the series, its popularity prompted Mattel to add more than 30 additional vehicles to the group by mid-year.

figure; and the Surf Crate, a woody-bodied hot rod that became an instant favorite with collectors.

Mattel arranged with Chrysler, the reigning king of concept cars, to reproduce two recent creations: the Dodge Charger R/T and the Dodge Power Wagon, a modern version of Dodge's classic 1940s heavy-duty pickup truck workhorse. In addition to black-painted headlight covers, the Charger even features twin gas caps, picked out in silver tampo.

"I like Hot Wheels cars because they are made of metal and the designs are neater [than other brands]. Matchbox has present-day cars but Hot Wheels has futuristic cars and neater cars like the Surf Crate and Deora II."

—Alex Stephens, age 12, Austin, Texas

In many ways, the 2000 First Editions Surf Crate sums up the Hot Wheels aesthetic. Mattel designers merged California surfing, hot rod wheels, a custom engine, and woody-bodied fantasy styling into one wild ride.

The 10 other four-car series were Seein' 3D Series, with numbers, stripes, and letters painted with a three-dimensional appearance; Attack Pack Series, featuring animal graphics; Circus On Wheels Series, wearing "Circus On Wheels" lettering; CD Customs Series, featuring cars with interactive CD-ROM graphics; Future Fleet 2000 Series, with black vehicles and deep-tinted plastic windows; Kung Fu Force, with Kung Fu action graphics; Mad Maniax Series, featuring a fire-eating caricatured face; Snack Time Series, with licensed logos of snack foods; Speed Blaster Series, with all cars featuring tampo-printed words like "speed," "performance," "power," and "attitude," (all current Hot Wheels marketing terms); and the Tony Hawk Skate series, which featured the well-known skateboarder's bird graphics.

Hot Wheels designs represent a uniquely American phenomenon and Mattel should be proud to have recorded the history of custom cars over the past 30-plus years. The brand will endure for decades if Mattel continues on the course it has followed since the beginning—an inspired creativity of design and a keen attention to quality construction. The company still uses generous amounts of metal while other toy companies have relied on more plastic parts. The designs remain fresh, sophisticated, and intriguing. For these reasons, collecting Hot Wheels cars remains a fascinating and satisfying hobby for children and adults.

Appendix

Buying Hot Wheels® Cars

With the popularity of Internet auctions such as eBay and Mobilia, it's tempting to go online in search of Hot Wheels cars. However, my experience, as well as that of many prominent collectors like Michael Strauss and Lance Joseph, has revealed that it is very risky to buy these toys over the Internet. Photographs, no matter how good, are not enough. This is because, unlike other toy cars that used opaque lacquer, early Hot Wheels cars (the Spectraflame years from 1968 to 1972) used transparent lacquer that exposed the flaws of the bare metal beneath. Over time, the metal has aged poorly on some cars, and produced dark spots (known in the hobby as "toning" and "shading") and flaws in the finish that are not always visible in photographs.

Post-1972 cars—the enamel years onward—are a safer bet to purchase without first seeing them. Chipped paint is more visible in photographs, and the risk of toning and shading is eliminated. Make sure the pictures show all angles of the car. If they do not, see if the seller will send more photos to you. Also, ask about any cracks in the glass, play-wear on the tires, and any flaw that might cause the car to be listed at less than mint condition. A 1-to-10 grading scale is often used when the buyer cannot see the toy in person. The best score is a 10, and it can be used for the car as well as its packaging.

Hot Wheels cars still in their original package are a slightly safer gamble if the collector is buying post Spectraflame-era cars and if mint-package condition isn't crucial. Never assume that a Spectraflame car in the package is in mint, like-new condition. These vehicles can age poorly inside their blisterpacks. Later-model cars are generally a safer bet, although sellers do not always mention minor nicks and creases in the packaging. Again, these flaws are hard to see in amateur photographs and if the collector wants perfect packaging as well, it is best to view the article in person.

The best place to buy Hot Wheels cars of any vintage is at swap meets and from established dealers. Find these through listings in magazines such as *Toy Cars & Models* and *Car Toy Collectibles*. Join one of the many independent Hot Wheels clubs around the nation and ask those collectors where to buy. Just type "hot wheels club" into any Internet search engine and dozens of choices will appear. If you do not have Internet access, subscribe to the Hot Wheels Newsletter listed below. The newsletter includes information on how to join one of the more than 50 chapters of their Collector's Club.

Resources

Espino, David. *Treasure Hunting Collectible Redlines*.
    Available from David Espino,
    P.O. Box 368,
    Pico Rivera, CA 90660-0368;
    www.redlinesonline.com

Parker, Bob. *The Complete Book of Hot Wheels 3rd ed*.
    Atglen, PA: Schiffer Publishing Ltd., 1998.
    ISBN: 0-7643-0612-X

Strauss, Michael Thomas. *Tomart's Price Guide to Hot Wheels Collectibles 4th ed*.
    Dayton, OH: Tomart Publications, 2000.
    ISBN: 0-914293-43-5

The Staff of Beckett Publications. *Hot Cars*.
    Dallas, TX: Beckett Publications, 1999.
    ISBN: 1-887432-69-8.

Hot Wheels Newsletter
26 Madera Ave.
San Carlos, CA 94070-2937
Contact: Michael Thomas Strauss

Price Guide

Page	Year	Model	Color	Value*
Cover	1998	'67 Camaro	blue (Race Team)	4
Cover	1997	'70 Plymouth Barracuda Convertible	lime	3
Frontis	2000	'53 Bel Air (Hot Wheels Collectibles)	light blue pearl	9
Title Page	1999	Ford Mustang Shelby GT350	white	30
7	1999	Lamborghini Miura	yellow	30
9	1970	2-Way Super-Charger		50
9	1995	Mean Green Passion	green	25
9	1969	Indy Eagle	green	24
9	1982	Sunagon	orange/tan	10
9	1970	King 'Kuda	blue	120
11	1968	Custom Camaro	orange	175
13	1970	Sand Crab	magenta	45
16	1968	Custom Fleetside	yellow	125
18	1970	Classic Nomad	pink	150
19	1968	Beatnik Bandit	magenta	75
19	1968	Custom Firebird	blue with blue interior	175
20	1968	Silhouette	purple	25
21	1969	TwinMill	light blue	125
22	1969	Beach Bomb	green	125
23	1969	Shelby Turbine	purple	30
24	1969	Custom Police Cruiser prototype	black and white	rare
24	1969	Classic '57 T-Bird	yellow	65
25	1970	Tow Truck	orange	50
27	1970	Heavy Chevy Club Kit car	chrome	85
28	1970	Snake funny car	yellow	90
28	1970	Mongoose funny car	red	85
29	1970	Jack "Rabbit" Special	white with Jack-in-the-Box decals	400
30	1970	Classic Nomad	olive	175
30	1970	Paddy Wagon	dark blue	30
30	1970	Red Baron	red	35
30	1971	S'Cool Bus	yellow	200
30	1970	Sand Crab	pink	90
30	1971	Ice "T"	yellow	65
31	1971	Mutt Mobile	gold	100
32	1971	Olds 442	red	500
33	1971	Classic Cord	gold	300
34	1971	Mongoose Rail Dragster	blue	100
34	1971	Snake Rail Dragster	white	100
36	1972	Ferrari 512 S	light green	100
37	1972	Open Fire	blue	450
38	1973	Superfine Turbine	dark blue	400
41	1973	Sweet 16	lime green	225
42	1974	Breakaway Bucket	blue	100
43	1974	Sir Rodney Roadster	green	500
43	1974	Baja Bruiser	orange	65
44	1975	Super Van Toy Fair vehicle	white	1,800
45	1975	Motocross 1	red	130
45	1975	Street Eater	yellow	110

Page	Year	Model	Color	Value*
46	1975	Ranger Rig	green	55
47	1975	P-911	yellow	75
47	1975	Chief's Special (Herfy's)	red	250
47	1975	Super Van (Herfy's/KGW Radio)	black	250
47	1975	Warpath (Herfy's)	white	300
48	1976	Corvette Stingray	chrome	90
49	1976	American Tipper	red, white, and blue	35
50	1976	Poison Pinto	light green	35
51	1977	'57 Chevy	red	75
52	1977	GMC Motor Home	orange	20
52	1977	'56 Hi-Tail Hauler	orange	50
53	1977	Odd Rod	plum	450
54	1978	'57 T-Bird	white	30
56	1978	Hot Bird	black	8
57	1978	Race Bait 308	red	12
57	1978	Packin' Pacer	yellow	8
58	1979	Captain America Van	white	75
58	1979	The Incredible Hulk	yellow	25
58	1981	Silver Surfer	chrome	18
59	1979	Spider-Man	black	15
60	1979	Auburn 852	red	8
60	1979	Greased Gremlin	red	25
61	1980	3-Window '34	red	15
62	1980	Hiway Hauler	white	20
63	1980	CAT Bulldozer	yellow	5
63	1980	CAT Dump Truck	yellow	5
64	1981	'37 Bugatti	black and red	6
65	1981	Bronco 4-Wheeler	black	8
65	1981	Dixie Challenger	orange	8
66	1982	'35 Classic Caddy	tan	8
68	2000	McDonald's Happy Meal car	dark blue	2
68	1982	Rapid Transit	white	30
69	1982	Aries Wagon	yellow	6
70	1982	Sunagon	orange and tan	10
71	1983	Jeep Scrambler	gray	35
72	1983	Renault Le Car	red	20
72	1983	Fiat Strada	gray	30
73	1983	'40s Ford 2-Door	black	15
73	1983	Classic Cobra	navy blue	20
74	1984	'65 Mustang Convertible	red	6
75	1984	Baja Bug	yellow	35
76	1984	Dream Van	metallic blue	20
77	1985	Fiero 2M4	white	8
78	1985	Nissan 300ZX	red	8
78	1986	Eevil Weevil	blue	5
78	1986	Double Demon	red	5
78	1986	Turboa	yellow	6
79	1987	Suzuki QuadRacer	yellow	4
80	1987	Ferrari Testarossa	black	18
81	1988	Lamborghini Countach	white	4
82	1988	Porsche 959	metallic red	8

Page	Year	Model	Color	Value*
83	1988	Talbot Lago	burgundy	8
84	1990	Purple Passion	purple metalflake	12
86	1989	Custom Corvette (Getty)	black	8
86	1989	Custom Corvette	metallic red	8
87	1989	'32 Ford Delivery	yellow	10
87	1989	Ferrari F40	red	3
87	1995	Ferrari F40	red	2
88	1990	BMW 323 California Custom	white and blue	12
89	1990	Mini Truck	turquoise	4
90	1991	Lamborghini Diablo	red	4
91	1993	Swingfire	blue metalflake and white	3
92	1992	'57 T-Bird "Gleam Team"	gold chrome	4
93	1992	Pro Circuit Hot Wheels Camaro	blue and white	7
93	1992	Pro Circuit Duracell Camaro	orange and black	6
94	1992	Chevy Lumina (minivan)	red	3
95	1993	Classic Nomad (25th Anniversary)	light blue	4
95	1993	Classic Nomad (25th Anniversary)	dark blue	5
96	1993	Dodge Viper RT/10	red	4
96	1999	Dodge Viper RT/10	metallic blue and white	2
97	1997	Oscar Mayer Wienermobile	red and tan	2
99	1994	Rigor Motor	red metalflake	8
100	1995	Dodge Ram 1500	aqua metalflake	4
103	1995	Camaro Racer	light blue chrome	10
104	1995	Mercedes-Benz Unimog	gray and orange	15
105	1995	Jaguar XJ220	white pearl	4
105	1995	Talbot Lago	blue pearl	2
105	1995	VW Bug	pink pearl	2
105	1995	Purple Passion	light purple pearl	4
106	1995	Lumina Stocker	light blue metalflake	4
106	1995	Lumina Stocker	dark blue metallic	3
107	1996	Corvette Coupe	green metalflake	2
109	1996	Radio Flyer Wagon	red	2
110	1996	Hummer	hot pink	2
111	1997	Hot Wheels Racing Kyle Petty Grand Prix	blue	2
111	2000	Hot Wheels Racing School Bus	dark blue	3
111	2000	Hot Wheels Racing Scorchin' Scooter	orange	3
111	2000	Hot Wheels Racing Suburban	black	3
112	2000	Hot Wheels Collectibles AMX	blue	6
113	1997	'59 Chevy Impala	plum metalflake	2
114	1997	'70 Plymouth Barracuda Convertible	light green	3
115	1997	'97 Corvette	green metalflake	2
116	1998	Go Kart	bright green	2
116	1999	Go Kart	orange	2
117	1998	Solar Eagle III	yellow	2
118	1998	Dairy Delivery	white pearl	2
120	1999	various Ferrari models	red	$2 each
121	1999	Tee'd Off	white	8
121	2000	Thomassima III	red metalflake	1
122	2000	'64 Lincoln Continental	white	1
123	2000	Surf Crate	purple metallic	1

*Values are for mint-condition cars with no packaging.

Index

'32 Ford Delivery, 85–87
'35 Classic Caddy, 67
'36 Cord sedan, 117
'37 Bugatti, 64
'37 Talbot Lago, 82, 83
'38 Phantom Corsair, 117
'40s Ford 2-Door, 73
'55 Chevy, 67, 68, 92
'55 Nomad, 90
'56 Flashsider, 94
'56 Ford truck, 118
'56 Hi-Tail Hauler, 52
'57 Chevy, 51, 92
'57 Classic T-Bird, 24
'57 T-Bird, 54, 55, 92
'59 Chevy Impala, 110, 113
'63 T-Bird, 113
'64 Lincoln Continental Convertible, 121, 122
'65 Impala lowrider, 113
'65 Mustang Convertible, 74, 75
'67 Camaro, 72
'67 Charger, 121
'70 Chevelle SS, 117
'70 Mustang Mach I, 113
'70 Plymouth Barracuda Convertible, 9
'70 Plymouth Barracuda, 110, 114
'70 Roadrunner, 113
'80s Corvette, 72
'80s Firebird, 72
'93 Camaro, 103
'97 Corvette, 115
2-Way Super-Charger, 9
3-Window '34 Ford, 61
Action Command series, 77
Airport Rescue fire truck, 65
Ambulance, 86
American Hauler, 48
American Tipper, 48, 49
AMX/2, 33
Aries Wagon, 69
Auburn 852, 58–60
Baja Breaker, 55
Baja Bruiser, 42, 43
Baja Bug, 75, 76
Battle Tank, 67
Beatnik Bandit, 19
Blown Camaro Z-28, 76
Blue Streak Series, 112
BMW 323, 88
Boss Hoss, 26, 27
Bradley, Harry, 13
Breakaway Bucket, 42
Bronco 4-Wheeler, 64, 65
Bye-Focal, 31
Bywayman, 58
California Customs series, 88
Camaro Convertible, 101
CAT Bulldozer, 63

CAT Dump Truck, 63
Chapparal 2G, 21
Chevy 1500 pickup truck, 108
Chevy Citation, 65
Chevy Lumina, 94
Chief's Special, 47
Classic Cobra, 72, 73
Classic Cord, 33
Classic Nomad, 18, 28, 30, 95
Cockney Cab, 31
Corgi Jr., 105–107, 110
Corvette Stingray, 48, 50
Cushenberry, Bill, 18
Custom Camaro, 11
Custom Corvette, 85, 86
Custom Firebird, 19
Custom Fleetside, 17
Custom Police Cruiser, 23, 24
Dairy Delivery, 113, 118
Daniel, Tom, 28, 30
Dark Rider Series, 104
Demolition Man Series, 96
Demon, 28
Dixie Challenger, 65
Dodge Omni 024, 65
Dodge Ram 1500, 100, 101
Dodge Rampage, 76, 77
Dodge Viper RT/10, 96, 97
Double Demon, 78, 79
Double Header, 39
Double Vision, 114
Dream Van, 76, 77
Eevil Weevil, 78, 79
Enamel Color Chart, 40
Evil Weevil, 31, 32
Express Lane, 114
Extras, 71
Fathom This, 114
Ferrari 250 Testa Rossa, 90
Ferrari 312P, 21
Ferrari 348, 90
Ferrari 355, 101
Ferrari 360 Modena, 116, 120
Ferrari 365 GTB/4 "Daytona," 120
Ferrari 456M, 116, 120
Ferrari 512S, 36
Ferrari F355 Spider, 116, 120
Ferrari F40, 86, 87
Ferrari F50 Berlinetta, 116, 120
Ferrari Testarossa, 80, 81
Fiat Strada, 77
Flat Out 442, 59
Formula 5000, 48
Funny Money, 37
Getty Oil Company promotional models, 85, 86
Gilford, Ira, 20, 26
Gleam Team Series, 91, 92
GMC Motorhome, 52
Go Kart, 113, 116

Golden Machines, 61
Grass Hopper, 31
Greased Gremlin, 59, 60
Gremlin Grinder, 44
Greyhound MC-8, 62
Gun Bucket, 48
Handler, Elliot, 12
Hare Splitter, 61
Heavy Chevy, 26, 27
Heavyweights Series, 25, 26, 33
Heroes Series, 58
Hi-Rakers, 61
Highway Patrol, 56
Hiway Hauler, 62, 92, 94
Hot Bird, 55, 56
Hot Curves Race Action Set, 11
Hot Ones, 64
Hot Rod magazine series, 122
Hot Seat, 114
Hot Wheels Club Kit, 26
Hot Wheels Collectibles, 109, 112
Hot Wheels Race Team, 112
Hydroplane, 102
Ice "T," 29, 30
Indy Eagle, 9
Jack "Rabbit" Special, 28, 29
Jaguar XJ220, 97, 105
Jay Leno collection, 6
Jeep Scrambler, 71, 74
Joseph, Lance, 9
Khaki Kooler, 48
King 'Kuda, 9, 26
LaBranch, Harvey, 12
Lamborghini Countach, 81, 82
Lamborghini Countach, 25th Anniversary, 110
Lamborghini Diablo, 90
Lamborghini Miura, 7
Lincoln Continental Mark III, 23
Marvel Comics, 58
Maserati Mistral, 22, 25
McDonald's promotional cars, 67, 68
Mean Green Passion, 9
Megadestroyer, 67
Mercedes 380 SEL, 69
Mercedes 540K, 67
Mercedes Unimog, 104
Mercedes-Benz 280 SL, 22, 25
Mercedes-Benz C-111, 36
Metal collector's button, 13
Mighty Maverick, 29
Mini Truck, 89
Mod Bod Series, 108, 110
Mongoose funny car, 27, 28, 33, 36, 40
Mongoose rail dragster, 34, 35
Motocross 1, 45
Mutt Mobile, 31, 32
Neet Streeter, 48

Newman, Howard, 12
Nissan 300ZX, 77, 78
No Fear racecar, 98
Odd Rod, 51, 53
Old Number 5, 64
Olds 442, 33
Open Fire, 36, 37
Oscar Mayer Wienermobile, 97, 98
Packin' Pacer, 56, 57
Paddy Wagon, 29, 30
Park 'n' Plates Series, 85
Pearl Driver Series, 104, 105
Phaeton, 118
Phantastique, 120
Poison Pinto, 50
Police Cruiser, 39
Pontiac Fiero 2M4, 77
Pontiac J-2000, 74
Porsche 911, 47
Porsche 917, 23
Porsche 959, 82
Pro Circuit Series, 91, 93
Pro Racing Series, 109, 112
Propper Chopper, 89
Purple Passion, 85, 88, 89, 105
Race Bait 308, 56, 57
Race Team Series, 104, 106, 115
Race Truck Series, 108
Racing Metals Series, 103
Radio Flyer Wagon, 108, 109
Ramp Truck, 91
Ranger Rig, 46
Rapid Transit, 68
Real Riders, 70, 71, 104
Red Baron, 29, 30
Rees, Howard, 29, 31
Renault Le Car, 72
Revealers, 95
Rigor Motor, 98, 99
Road King, 42
Road Rocket, 115
Rocket-Bye-Baby, 32
Rolls-Royce Silver Shadow, 22, 25
Roth, Ed "Big Daddy," 18
Royal Flash, 59
Ruby Red Passion, 92
Ryan, Jack, 12
S'Cool Bus, 29, 30
Sand Crab, 13, 29, 30
Scene Machines, 58
School Bus, 86
Science Friction, 56
Scorchin' Scooter, 110
Seasider, 29
Sharkruiser, 79
Shelby GT350, 3, 4
Shelby Turbine, 23
Shell Oil promotional cars, 40
Short Order, 31
Side Kick, 37

Silhouette, 20
Sir Rodney Roadster, 42, 43
Six Shooter, 32
Sky Show Deora, 28
Sky Show Fleetside, 28
Snake funny car, 27, 28, 33, 36, 40, 56, 69
Snake rail dragster, 34, 35
Sol-Aire CX4, 75
Solar Eagle III, 114, 117
Spectraflame Colors, 15, 17
Speed Demons, 78, 79
Spoilers Series, 26, 27
Staff Car, 50
Stagefright, 56
Strauss, Michael Thomas, 33, 41, 50
Street Beast, 91
Street Eater, 45
Street Roader, 86
Strip Tease, 32
Stutz Blackhawk, 63
Sunagon, 9, 69, 70
Super California Customs, 90
Super Chromes, 58
Super Van, 44, 47
Superfine Turbine, 38, 39
Surf Crate, 123
Suzuki QuadRacer, 79, 80
Sweet 16, 39, 41
Swingfire, 91
T-4-2, 31, 32
Tail Dragger, 113
Talbot Lago, 105
Tam, Paul, 29, 31, 36, 39
Tattoo Machines, 95, 96
Tee'd Off, 118, 121
Thomassima III, 120, 121
Tow Truck, 25
Track T, 118
Turboa, 78, 79
TwinMill, 20, 21
Upfront 924, 59
Vampyra, 79
Vetty Funny, 59
Vintage Collection, 98
Virtual Collection, 122
Volkswagen Beach Bomb, 20–22
VW Bug, 86, 105
VW Bus funny car, 107
Wagner, Jim, 101, 113
Warpath, 47
Whatta Drag, 114
Wheels, types, 14
White Ice Series, 112
Wood, Larry, 29, 31, 37, 39
Workhorses, 62, 62
Xploder, 40
Z Whiz, 51